Gabrielle trained as an actress, gaining a BA (Hons) Acting
for Film and Television at Arts Educational Schools London.
Her hobbies include embarrassing her parents, putting her
foot in it, repulsing the entire male population and forgetting
to shave her legs.

LUSH

A TRUE STORY, SOAKED IN GIN

Gabrielle Fernie

sphere

SPHERE

First published in Great Britain in 2018 by Sphere

1 3 5 7 9 10 8 6 4 2

A CIP catalogue record for this book
is available from the British Library.

ISBN 978-0-7515-7008-3

Typeset in Dante by M Rules
Printed and bound in Great Britain by
Clays Ltd, Elcograf S.p.A.

Papers used by Sphere are from well-managed forests
and other responsible sources.

Sphere
An imprint of
Little, Brown Book Group
Carmelite House
50 Victoria Embankment
London EC4Y 0DZ

An Hachette UK Company
www.hachette.co.uk

www.littlebrown.co.uk

To anyone who's ever been told 'You were really embarrassing last night'.

LUSH

A TRUE STORY, SOAKED IN GIN

1

The Engagement

It is the hottest day of the year and I am having a wax. I do not mean this in the conventional sense. I am not in a beauty parlour. There is no calming pipe music playing. I am not on all fours while an Icelandic woman named Helga pulls apart my arse cheeks so that she can 'really get to the nooks and crannies'. No.

I am sitting bare-legged on our leather sofa, and every time I stand up, the hairs on my thighs stay stuck to it. My legs are slowly but surely becoming waxed smooth. It is a fascinating yet traumatic experience. And our once-leather couch has now started to take on a new, furry texture. Like velvet. Or suede.

Bloody cut my head off and shove it up Jack Frost's arse, *I'm hot*. I have an industrial-sized fan on, with which I have learned to synchronise my smoking. Every time the fan swings towards me I must quickly inhale, then rapidly duck and puff as it bears right, so the smoke isn't blown back in my face, blinding me. It is a slick, choreographed workout. I think I might actually be developing abs.

To make matters worse, I am currently in the midst of the hangover from hell. I'm not talking the bearable kind, where you pop a couple of painkillers, un-tag the photo of you shitting in a bus shelter and head off for brunch with the girls. Oh no. We are talking the type of hangover sent by Lucifer himself. The sort where every limb feels like it's been through a Christmas-tree shredder. Like a small family of possums have curled up and died in your mouth. Like a group of primary school children have just learned to make scrambled eggs WITH YOUR BRAIN.

Why do I insist on doing this to myself? Why, why, why?!

To add to this Greek tragedy of pain and woe, I have just this morning received some highly distressing news: MY BEST FRIEND EMMA HAS GOT ENGAGED.

The fact that we are both twenty-three years old, grew

up in the same small Welsh town, attended the same school, have had almost identical upbringings and yet she is currently engaged to the love of her life while I sit on the shelf like a jar of stale fucking Bovril could be seen as a sore point. But luckily I am above all that.

She gets to spend the next few months planning a beautiful wedding. I have recently discovered that my breasts float in the bath. She will be relaxing this summer, honeymooning on a tropical beach. I shall be on the streets of Shoreditch having a conversation with a wheelie bin.

As I say, I'VE MADE MY PEACE WITH IT.

After dropping out of her nursing degree at Swansea University (I don't think she ever got over the trauma of having to shave an elderly lady's pubes on her first day), Emma decided to stay on in our home town to work at her family's darts company. Positioned on the reception desk, she now happily spends her days chatting on Facebook, researching boob jobs and dramatically rolling her eyes at anyone who dares to come in and order darts.

I met Emma at the tender age of three, while attending our local village nursery. With her freckled face and her vibrant bob of ginger hair (which she would later in life fiercely defend as being strawberry blonde, before dyeing it red, brown and eventually black), she gave off a distinct air of fun and naughtiness. I clocked her immediately on that first day and doggedly followed her round the Wendy house, soft-play area and sandpit until we became best friends.

Our friendship often led me into trouble. In Year 4, Emma

snuck a sex education book into school, stolen from her mother's shelf. Looking back, it was a rather strange and perverted read. 'The penis stands up straight like a soldier!' it explained, alongside a cartoon of a penis wearing a soldier's hat and winking. Needless to say, the book was quickly confiscated by our teacher and our parents were called. Then there was the time she invented a game that involved sliding under the partitions of the girls' toilet cubicles and locking all the doors from the inside. Unfortunately, our (slightly larger) friend Mollie got stuck under one of the partitions, resulting in the head teacher having to pull her out by her legs.

Things did not improve much in secondary school. Emma would make me laugh so much in lessons (particularly while reading aloud in religious studies) that I would snort like a highly amused pig, causing both of us to be sent out of the classroom and ordered to face the wall. It is also astonishing that we passed all of our exams without facing expulsion, due to the fact that our entire GCSE Welsh oral exam was pre-written on our inner thighs.

Sleepovers together would always involve some crazy activity. We once called a live sex line (found in the back of *Cosmo*) and were so shocked and horrified by the old creep at the other end that we hung up in silence before collapsing into screams of laughter. Or there was the night when we decided at 1 a.m. that we would use our new Nokia 3410s to call some of the boys we fancied from our year. Emma had the hots for a boy called Chris, and I was amazed to discover I had his number in my phone. After making about seven calls, all of which were answered by a harassed woman ('Hello, this is Gabrielle, may I speak to Chris, please?' 'Yes, Gabrielle, this IS Chris'), I eventually twigged that I was actually calling Christine, our forty-two-year-old next-door neighbour, who my mother had to placate the next morning with a bunch of flowers.

But while Emma has frequently got me into trouble, she is also the most down-to-earth and good-hearted person I know – forever taking the piss out of herself and seeing the funny side in the direst of situations. She is the one girl who can match me in drink, jokes and tales of debauchery, and I regard her as the dearest of all my friends.

We hadn't spoken in several weeks, so when I saw her name pop up, I scrabbled for my ringing mobile in delight.

'Pegleg!'

'Bitchtits!' cried Emma. 'I've got some exciting news for you.'

(Note: the nicknames Pegleg and Bitchtits stem from a girls' holiday we took to Magaluf in 2010, along with the entire population of Bridgend: hundreds of rowdy Welsh eighteen-year-olds keen to drink their own body weight, sleep with strangers and stick fireworks up their arses. One night Emma sprained her ankle badly and really should have gone to A&E. However, we chose not to take that option – wouldn't want to waste precious drinking time, WAHEY! Instead we decided to fashion her a home-made splint out of ripped-up bed sheets, Kirby grips and twigs. The result was outstanding – Emma mincing around the clubs in a little minidress with a gigantic club foot. I don't remember how I acquired the name Bitchtits, but I suspect it had something to do with my penchant for taking my bra off in clubs and lassoing it around my head. Or the time I whipped both my breasts out on the dance floor and banged them together like a pair of bellows.)

'Oh God,' I said. 'I've missed you! There's so much to fill you in on. I slept with this man called Wayne last week and left a massive fake-tan stain on his sheets. I had to spend twenty minutes the next morning convincing him that I hadn't soiled myself.'

'Gabs—'

'Also, I've discovered that when I'm lying on my bed reading a book and my legs are in the perfect position, I can make myself queef on demand. Not a fart – an *actual* queef. Sometimes at different pitches. Is this normal? Can you do it?'

'Gabs, I'm engaged.'

Pause. A smile froze on my face.

'Engaged in what? A hobby?'

'I'm engaged to be married, Gabs.'

'Married . . . to Sam?'

'Yes, obviously Sam. Yes.'

I couldn't exactly pinpoint what I was feeling at that moment, but I became vaguely aware of a strangled scream escaping from my body. Similar to the sound of foxes mating.

'Gabs, are you okay?'

'Me? ME?!' I realised my voice sounded absurdly high-pitched. 'Oh God, I'm fine! More than fine, actually, I'm THRILLED! Thrilled for you!'

'Really? Oh, thank God! I was a bit scared to tell you because of . . . well, you know. The place you're in right now.'

'What place would that be, Emma? Hmm? A slap-my-arse-and-call-me-Sandra-because-I'M-AS-FINE-AS-A-WHISTLE place?'

'Well, you know. You mentioned things weren't going particularly well, with work and dating and that.'

'Oh, don't be silly! Everything is brilliant! Marvellous, in fact! My life is ticking along like a . . . like a jolly egg-timer.'

I laughed manically and lit another fag.

'There was another thing,' she said. 'I wondered whether you would like to be my bridesmaid?'

A blast of love and emotion slapped me in the face like a wet fish. Maid of honour at my best friend's wedding! Of course she would ask me. *Of course.* Twenty years of friendship, from sharing a bath as toddlers to holding each other's hair back while we puked up Bacardi Breezers at the sixth-form party. All leading up to this moment.

I hastily fanned away my tears with the nearest Jehovah's Witness leaflet.

'Oh God, Ems. I would love to. LOVE TO. You will seriously not regret this. I'm going to be the best maid of honour who ever lived. You're going to have an ungodly hen do with at least four strippers and—'

'Oh. Actually, Gabs, I've asked Nat to be maid of honour. Hope you don't mind. It's just, you know, she's around a lot more and . . .'

A lump of bile rose in my throat.

Oh no. Oh please God, no. Anyone but Natasha *fucking* Jones.

My relationship with Natasha has always been a fractious one. We attended primary school together, where we spent six years in a constant battle for Emma's affections. (I mean this in a childish, best-friendy sort of way – we were not a trio of budding young lesbians.)

It started with friendship necklaces. Do you remember those bloody things? Silver hearts sawn in two, which when joined together spelled something like 'FRIENDS FOREVER'. Or 'BESTIES 4 LYFE'. The fact that the cheap metal made your neck go green after fourteen hours of wear, resulting in a severed head/Frankenstein's monster look, did not matter. They were a status symbol. A sign of ownership. A sign of love.

Well, Natasha bought a pair of such necklaces for her and Emma in Year 5, when we were ten years old. It was a deliberate tactical move. One designed to shove me out the way and force me to befriend someone like Jamie Billington, who wore Velcro shoes and shoved pencils up his nose. They wore the necklaces all day long, half-strangling themselves every hour or so to join the pieces together and scream with delight.

I too did a lot of screaming that day. At home, at the kitchen table, as I caterwauled to my mother at this act of barbarity and betrayal. My mother, quite reasonably, suggested that I should simply ignore the necklaces. True friendship, she explained, was not defined by a cheap piece of metal tied around your neck. It was made from much greater things: loyalty, trust and love.

I quietly took in her words and decided to handle the situation with wisdom and maturity beyond my years.

I WENT OUT AND BOUGHT A PAIR OF NECKLACES OF MY OWN, one of which I presented to Emma the following morning.

Although we eventually grew out of the friendship necklaces (had we worn them much longer we would all have run the risk of developing dermatitis), the rivalry between me and Natasha continued throughout our childhood and teenage years. A catalogue of exclusive sleepovers, inside jokes and bitter resentment.

Eventually, having left secondary school and gone our separate ways to university and college, we reached a sort of grudging friendship. The three of us would meet up in the holidays and things seemed fine. Pleasant, even. Natasha and I would never be the best of friends, but we had attained a level of mutual understanding. We had both, finally, grown up.

Well, I can tell you now, THAT SHIP HAS FUCKING WELL SAILED!

How dare Emma pick Nat? How *dare* she?! Natasha Jones, the most CRASHING BORE to ever grace the streets of Cardiff? A girl with all the personality of a battered cod? Okay, okay – maybe not a battered cod. That would be unfair to the cod.

Natasha showcases a very wholesome image of herself. Each day her Facebook and Instagram feeds are filled with photos of her #blessed life: gym selfies with her beefcake of a boyfriend, both tanned, toned and honed to loathsome perfection; snaps of her smashed avocado, poached egg and sourdough brunch; nights out standing next to her perfectly manicured and simpering friends, their smiles frozen on their Botoxed faces. These photos will often be accompanied by a nauseating 'motivational' quote, such as: 'Today I will do what others won't, so tomorrow I can do what others can't.' Oh, fuck off.

They are a stark contrast to my own Facebook and Instagram photos, which normally involve me puking behind a car on a night out or standing in a bar with an ice bucket on my head.

The thing is, although Natasha has grown into a vaguely tolerable if nauseating individual, I cannot forgive her for those years of apparent bullying and spitefulness in primary school. Parties at her house that I was not invited to. Or parties at her house which I *was* invited to but where she'd persuade everyone to hide from me, screaming and giggling round the house. 'Accidentally' bashing past me in corridors. Basically being the whispering, sniggering RINGLEADER who made the early years of my life a perfect misery.

Suddenly I was ten years old again – tearful, petulant and ready to punch a wall. Oh yes, I'm sure she'll throw you a blinding hen do, Emma. BLINDING. We'll probably spend the night playing tiddlywinks and then bleaching each other's arseholes. But somehow, dredging up every ounce of strength and maturity I possessed, I managed to keep it together.

'That's great!' I croaked. 'Really great. I'm sure she'll do a cracking job.'

I could hear Emma's relief down the phone.

'Thanks *so* much, Gabs. Knew you'd be cool about it. Anyway, I've gotta dash and start fake-tanning. Sam's parents are taking us out later to that new Thai place in Cardiff Bay. What are you up to tonight?'

I grimly surveyed the polystyrene container on the kitchen floor holding the contents of last night's half-eaten kebab.

'Oh, you know! The same, really. May go out for a fancy dinner with … um … one of my many suitors. Honestly, I can't keep up with them all. I feel like the Pied Piper of Penis!'

'Ha ha, that's the spirit! Well, speak to you soon, Gabs. Lots of love.'

'Lots of love too! And congrats!'

We hung up. I sat silently for a moment.

Well, there we have it. The first of the gang to get married. Pfft. Rather her than me. Perhaps she'd get a perm. Or start going to oven-glove conventions.

Shakily, I took a drag from my cigarette and watched two pigeons hump on the windowsill outside.

Then I burst into tears.

2

Drama Fool

Life has not always been this way. I was raised as a proper country bumpkin. That's right – a potato-digging, muck-spreading clodhopper. The first nineteen years of my life were spent in a tiny rural village in South Wales, where the annual highlights included maypole dancing and a fiercely competitive swede-rolling contest. While others filled their teenage years with vodka, house parties and fumbling sex, I led a sheltered and blissful existence of farm work, music lessons and amateur dramatics.

'Why would I choose to drink alcohol when I can get fresh milk from our very own cow?!'

'You're all going to the park to do balloons and poppers? Oh goody, I LOVE party poppers! I'll bring the paper hats. And I can make a balloon stegosaurus!'

'Sorry, John, it's really sweet of you to invite me to the party tonight, but Mum's making me my favourite casserole. With extra dumplings!'

I drove a tractor. I sang in the church choir. I owned a pet pig. (Pixie was a birthday present from my parents turned hideously wrong. She started out as a micropig. A sweet, cuddly little thing that I could tuck under my arm and dress up in frilly bonnets. Six months later she had inexplicably become the size of a small combine harvester. Two feet tall and four feet long, nudging ten stone, she is an aggressive, belligerent TYRANT. Having destroyed the downstairs of our house by charging at walls and attacking the hardwood flooring, she was relegated to a life in the garden, where she now merrily spends her days rolling in her own shit and snarling at the postman.)

I didn't care for parties or clubs and would rather make my own fun on a Saturday night, such as shearing a few sheep or farting in the bath and pretending it was a jacuzzi.

But then, at the age of nineteen, I moved to London to start a degree at drama school. And everything changed.

Lots of successful actors irritatingly describe acting as a career that they unexpectedly 'fell into'. Like skidding and landing on top of an incredibly lucrative dog turd.

'Oh, I'd always planned on going to university to study economics,' they trill while being interviewed about their first starring role in some BBC period drama. 'And then one day my uncle [insert name of massively famous actor here] dragged me along for this casting and the next minute BAM! Before I know it, I'm signed to United Agents and jetting off to start filming in LA.'

Well, it didn't happen that way for me. And it never will happen that way for me either, being the daughter of a teacher mother and a microbiologist father. (A very well-respected microbiologist, as he never tires of reminding me, who could easily have given me a leg up in my career had my interests lain not in theatre but in microsporidia fungi.) But despite my lack of well-connected thespian relatives, ever since the age of six, when I was cast as Mary in the school nativity, I knew that acting was what I wanted to do.

As far as first roles go, my portrayal of Mary wasn't a huge success. First, I brought Cabbage Patch doll Jesus on three scenes too early, clutching him possessively to my chest as the Angel Gabriel delivered the news that God had made me with child. The result was less shocked, innocent virgin and more that of a pissed-off single mother on Jeremy Kyle. ('Who is this God, then, eh? You don' mean Godfrey from down the Fox an' Hounds? I swear, Jezza, we 'ad a fumble in the disabled loo but nuffin' else, an' I'll do the DNA test t'prove it.')

Secondly, I was not the most angelic-looking of children. I have been cursed with an almightily large forehead (we're talking seven fingers here), which throughout my life I have attempted to hide behind a heavy fringe. With my hair scraped back by my home-made blue flannel headdress, I unfortunately bore a stark resemblance to Mrs Potato Head. Or a large thumb.

To add insult to injury, I was at this age also missing my two front teeth, giving me a very pronounced comedy lisp. My parents have a video recording of the final stable scene, where, in a rather high-handed and dictatorial way, I turned to the three wise men and delivered the line 'HITH NAME ITH JETHUTH AND HE SHALL BE THE THON OF GOD.' Then, in a moment of pure improvisation, I gestured to the proffered bottle of frankincense and added, 'Put the prethents over there, pleathe.'

The flame inside me had been lit.

I have always been something of an attention-seeker. An exhibitionist, if you like. As will become clear, I possess a lethal mixture of very few inhibitions and a complete lack of decorum, something that my parents realised when I was just three years of age. One day, I dragged my empty toy box to their bedroom door and sat in it, naked as a jaybird, then proceeded to lie on my back with my legs pulled up over my head and shout, 'SPECIAL DELIVERY! IT'S YOUR CHRISTMAS TURKEY!'

I also took to hiding items around the house, such as my parents' keys, or my brother's new stationery set, just so that

I could make an extravagant show of having found them. I remember once my brother had his friend Andy over. Determined to show off to him and catch his 'special attention', I decided to colour my entire face in with a purple felt-tip pen. This, in hindsight, is a clear indication of the disastrous approach to flirting that would plague me later in life.

Anyway, from my starring role as Dictator Mary, I went on to play roles outside of school, in various amateur dramatic companies. My first was as Dorothy in the village production of *The Wizard of Oz*. This, I hasten to add, was a rather warped, modern version, written by one of our local residents. Instead of the Tin Man, the Scarecrow and the Lion, Dorothy was met by David Beckham, Elvis Presley and Laurence Llewelyn-Bowen. And at the start of the play, instead of singing the timeless, beautiful song 'Somewhere Over The Rainbow', I was made to sing Michael Jackson's 'Black Or White', with a topical change of lyrics:

> *I took my Toto for a walk in the rain.*
> *And when it's sunny then the colour's the same.*
> *But I believe in miracles and a miracle might*
> *   happen tonight!*
> *But we're living in Kansas City and in Kansas it's just*
> *   black and white.*

As you can imagine, it was a real crowd-pleaser.

As I got older, my roles became somewhat meatier, including Eliza Doolittle in *My Fair Lady* and Wendla in *Spring Awakening*, where my poor parents had to watch my character lose her virginity on stage and beg to be beaten on the arse with a stick.

On stage, I was on an emotional roller coaster. By embodying these characters I was experiencing dizzying highs and lows that I could never hope to replicate in my own rather humdrum life. The world was my oyster. I was a giant koi carp in a tiny village pond and ready to take the professional acting world by storm.

And then I went to drama school.

I must clarify that I was not one of those talented individuals who are snapped up by somewhere like RADA on their first audition. I was instead forced to take a gap year, having received rejections from every drama school in the country in my first round of trying.

The auditions themselves can only be described as soul-destroying.

The suggestion that the acting industry is heavily skewed towards the privileged begins to ring true when you realise that even auditioning at drama school now costs each applicant upwards of fifty pounds. Factor in train fares, tube tickets and several overpriced lattes and you are talking a hell of a bloody lot of money.

So receiving an impersonal three-sentence rejection letter a couple of days later in the post, with absolutely no explanation or feedback, is something of a kick in the teeth. No, not a kick in the teeth. It is an unconcerned wallop in your giant, hope-filled testicles. (I hasten to clarify that I do not actually possess testicles. My giant, hope-filled vagina, then.)

Worse than the rejection letter is 'the list'. Some schools choose to publicly read out, on the day, the names of those who have made it through to the next round that afternoon and those who need to leave. Meaning that rejects such as me are faced with the excruciating task of gathering up our bags and vacating the building, simultaneously trying not to burst into tears or punch any of the successful applicants on the way out.

The auditions themselves often involve a ghastly group-activity section, where the crowd of about twenty hopeful auditionees are made to engage in an assortment of warm-up games. These often include 'Zip Zap Boing' (the hideousness of this game can be summed up in two words: INVISIBLE BALL) or prancing around the room to jungle music, pretending to be a crowd of apes.

My favourite audition anecdote comes from my friend Tom. One by one the group he was in were asked to open an imaginary door and react to a scene of horror before them.

'What do you see?' the panel asked the first girl.

'I see . . . I see poverty!' she cried, melodramatically shuddering and shielding her eyes. 'Poverty and starving children!'

'Good, good.' The panel all nodded, scribbling notes on their pads.

The second applicant went up.

'I see DEATH,' he hollered. 'Death coming towards me like a vast raincloud, showering the human race with oblivion!'

'Very nice,' nodded the panel.

Then it was Tom's turn. He walked forward and opened the imaginary door.

'AAARGH!' he screamed.

'What do you see, Tom?' asked the panel, leaning forward in interest.

'I've just walked in on my parents having sex,' he replied.

Although this is quite clearly comedy gold, he did not receive a callback.

The second half of the audition would normally then involve individually performing two contrasting monologues to the panel. For my first monologue, on the day of my very first audition, I chose to play the rather ambitious and totally unsuitable role of Queen Margaret from Shakespeare's *King Henry VI*.

Having up until this point been completely submerged in the world of amateur dramatics, I believed no performance, no matter how great or small, to be complete without the aid of props. Any actor worth their salt wouldn't be seen DEAD on stage without their trusty suitcase of fake swords, spud guns and comedy banana skins!

Therefore, on the poignant line 'Look, York. I stain'd this napkin with the blood that valiant Clifford, with his rapier's point, made issue from the bosom of the boy', I decided to dazzle them all by conjuring a bloodstained napkin from my sleeve, in the manner of a murderous magician.

Shortly before my turn in front of the panel, I realised that I had left said napkin on the train while practising my mono-logue (much to the horror of my fellow passengers, I'm sure).

In a moment of pure madness, I decided instead to produce several sheets of loo roll from my sleeve, hastily grabbed from the toilets and scribbled over with a red biro.

The sheets of paper, of course, tore in half upon being pulled out, creating a cloud of dust and floating pathetically to the floor while the panel stared in stunned disbelief. I imagine it is now a horror story they tell their first-year students.

Thankfully, having learned my lesson first time round, my second year of auditions was somewhat more of a success, and I gained a place (although not my first, second, third or even fifth choice) at a very well-respected school to study a three-year degree in acting. I had finally done it. FAME AND FORTUNE BECKONED!

Little did I know that it was all to go tits-up from here (or tits-down, to be more accurate). Let's start with my fellow students. First impressions? All the girls in my year were *tiny*. Dainty, waif-like little creatures who went to the gym every evening and pushed around plates of salad at lunch. The last gym I had attended was 'Jungle Jim's' for my tenth birthday, where I devoured a lunch of cupcakes and chips and then had a panic attack when I got stuck in the ball pit.

I have felt chubby my whole life. A little on the portly side, if you will. But it soon became clear on my first day at drama school that I was *not* chubby. Far from it, in fact. I was gargantuan. A full-on, bearish BUTTERBALL.

Luckily I made three very good friends at drama school: Robyn, Alice and Katie. From completely different walks of life, we were united by the fact that we found the whole drama school process to be faintly ridiculous and the rest of our year group completely intolerable. I thought *I* was a bit of a drama queen, but dear God, these other students took the biscuit (or rather, didn't take the biscuit. Took the kale, perhaps). There would be daily temper tantrums. Actual hysterical outbursts during classes where grown men and women would start crying and storm out, screaming that they just COULDN'T COPE with the emotional strain of it all.

I mean, we are not talking particularly stressful activities here. Watching, aged eleven, as your horse is castrated, and then the vet handing you the testicles 'for the dog to chew'… THAT is stressful. Spending an hour's physical practice class pretending to be a shoal of fish or a piece of bamboo is not.

Within around six months of arriving in London, I found myself slowly transforming into a creature I didn't recognise. Perhaps it was the people surrounding me, perhaps it was the immense culture shock of city life, but I can summarise my gradual decline from rural plough jockey to wayward wastrel in four simple categories: cigarettes, booze, meat and men.

Let us start with the fags.

Having previously written off smoking as a filthy habit reserved for toothless old hillbillies and my uncle Stanley, my opinion started to change when I hit London.

Nearly everybody at drama school smoked. As soon as classes ended, the entire college would swarm to socialise in the smoking area and I would be left blinking and clean-lunged in the corridor. It quickly became apparent that if I didn't learn to suckle on the devil's teat, then I was going to graduate after three years having made absolutely no friends at all.

And it wasn't just drama school. Wherever I went in London, be it pubs, clubs or bars, all the seemingly interesting people – and more to the point, the FIT MEN – were outside, flirting, chatting and snogging in a heady cloud of nicotine. I soon realised that this glorious little death stick was my one-way ticket to a giant cockfest. And I was diving in head-first.

Being a smoking novice, there were some slight mishaps along the way. Like the time I borrowed a guy's lighter, locking eyes over the flame in what I hoped was a sultry manner, and inadvertently set my fringe alight. Or the occasion when I rolled a cigarette so loose and baggy that I managed to actually inhale the filter.

But in spite of these early setbacks, I successfully and stupidly developed a complete nicotine addiction. And then came stage two: the drinking. After an entirely sober nineteen years in which the sum total of my alcohol consumption amounted to a portion of sherry trifle each Christmas, I dived into the sea of booze with all the enthusiasm of a newborn otter.

My main weakness was for gin. Oh those sweet, sweet juniper berries. Mother's ruin! Vera Lynn! Like some lardy eighteenth-century prostitute on Gin Lane, I soon found myself working through a small bottle of Gordon's a week. Which very quickly turned into a big bottle and a couple of small bottles. These were often drunk alone in my bedroom, with me crying over something ridiculous on the television like the Cesar dog food advert.

My drinking started to somewhat define me amongst my peers.

'Which one is Gabby?'

'Oh, you know, the tubby one in second year who drank six glasses of mulled wine and slid down the stairs in a pair of oven mitts.' (I hasten to add that this did not happen during school time, but afterwards in the comfort of my shared flat. Unfortunately the incident was filmed and played on the big screen at the graduation ball.)

Then, perhaps most surprisingly of all, came the meat-eating.

I grew up in a family of vegetarians. There was actually one stage at which my older brother turned us all vegan, so we were forced into drinking rice milk and couldn't eat Cheerios because the honey involved cruelty to bees. It remains one of the most traumatic periods of my life. (I should point out that my brother was heavily influenced at the time by his meek, mild TREE-HUGGER of a girlfriend, who didn't believe in drinking and used to carry a trowel in her handbag so she could dig a hole and shit in the woods. We never quite got along.)

Anyway, being a big animal lover, I trundled along quite nicely as a vegetarian over the years.

'Why would I want to eat a cow? So sweet! So furry!'

'Awww, look at that adorable chicken! LET ME PICK IT UP AND GIVE IT A GIANT KISSY!'

But around two years into my London life, something . . . happened. Something dark. Something disturbing. It would turn midnight, I'd have sunk a few bottles of gin and I'd start to get these . . . how can I put this delicately? RAW-BLOODED MEAT CRAVINGS.

It became a dirty secret. Ostentatiously picking off the pieces of pepperoni from a shared pizza, then secreting them in my handbag to gorge on later. Leaving the flat under cover of darkness (if I had owned a balaclava I would have worn it) to get my sick thrills at the local kebab shop.

Things truly hit a low point when I returned to my parents' house for Christmas and went out clubbing with the girls. Oh, that night. God forgive that fateful night. Stumbling home at 4 a.m., wild-eyed and smelling of tequila, I headed to the kitchen looking for my fix. Meat . . . where in the name of God was I going to find any meat?!

And then it hit me. Freddie. Our puppy. Our adorable little cocker spaniel puppy. He was in the process of being trained and there were some meaty puppy-training treats in the fridge. (You thought I was going to say that I ate Freddie, didn't you?)

So I did it. Sitting at the kitchen table, *I ate Freddie's puppy-training treats*. They were described as containing 'meat-based matter'. I can't quite bring myself to think of what that matter might have been.

Morning came and my mother wandered out of the kitchen looking perplexed. 'Somebody's taken all of Freddie's training treats!' she said.

'HEAVENS TO BETSY!' I replied, trying to match her astonished tone and stifle a meat-based-matter burp.

We never did get to the bottom of where Freddie's treats went. My suggestion that perhaps he opened the fridge and helped himself – 'Good God, the dog's a genius, Mother!' – wasn't met with much enthusiasm.

And so, having successfully converted to the status of nicotine-ridden, booze-sodden carnivore, came the final stage of my demise. MEN. Or, more accurately, one-night stands.

As a late bloomer, I didn't really start dating till the age of eighteen. I lost my virginity to my first boyfriend in his garden shed, with an episode of *The Inbetweeners* playing in the background. (As I say, a VERY late bloomer.) There was a slightly awkward moment where, halfway through, he asked me, 'You 'kay?', and I misheard it as 'You're gay' and burst into tears. But apart from that, my limited dating history was pretty tame and uneventful.

Up until I went to drama school, I had slept with only two men; within a year of living in London I had tripled my figures. Two years down the line I had (rather appropriately) sextupled them.

One guy who became a bit more than a one-night stand was a comedian I met at a New Year's Eve house party. Due to his celebrity status (albeit D-list), I shall respect his privacy by renaming him Ryan. He was a large, hairy, egotistical man, who saw himself as the absolute cat's pyjamas. Although I was initially repulsed by his advances, he eventually wore me down, via a series of witty Facebook messages, to agreeing to meet him for a drink.

Laughter has always been the way to my heart. Give me Mr Blobby over Brad Pitt any day. And somehow, after several dates, Ryan's whimsical anecdotes and amusing one-liners managed to completely win me over. (I now realise that comedians are constantly trying out new material for shows, making me less of a girlfriend and more a star-stuck, gullible guinea pig.) After about date five, however, by which point he'd had his 'wicked way' several times, he completely lost interest.

It's tragic, looking back on it now. I would spend all my savings on a carefully constructed outfit from Topshop (or, let's be honest, Primark), then sit waiting in a bar for him, only for him to text after forty minutes saying he'd been 'held up filming' and wouldn't be able to see me after all.

Soon I actually found myself stalking his Twitter feed, working out which part of the country he was performing in and when he'd be back in London to possibly see me. Eventually, having painfully got the message, I came home to Wales for the weekend, utterly deflated and depressed.

This is when I relate to you one of the greatest acts of love one's parents could ever show to their dejected daughter.

Knowing Ryan to be large, fat and hairy, they went to the Cardiff Hamleys store and bought a life-sized cuddly stuffed-toy gorilla. When I returned to London on the Monday, I received an email from my dad with the subject: 'We still love you!'

Attached were photos of the gorilla (hereafter known as Nigel) partaking in a number of 'leisure activities' around the house. For example, propped up against the kitchen counter, Dad's chef's hat on his head and chopping up bananas. Or sat wearing a pair of sunglasses, a suitcase in each hand, presumably about to set off on holiday.

As you can see, they are the most stark raving mad and brilliant of parents.

Somehow I survived the three years at drama school. I mean, it wasn't *all* bad. In spite of the mania, I discovered a love of comedy and started doing stand-up in my spare time. It turned out that while my drama school classmates were horrified by my tales of drinking and one-night stands, audiences of complete strangers absolutely loved them.

'I met a guy last Saturday in a club and asked him to come home with me,' I once cheerfully admitted to a crowd. 'His reply was, "Ummm. I dunno. Maybe. Do you have an iPhone charger?"' The audience laughed and groaned in mutual sympathy.

'And instead of walking away in revulsion, I found myself helpfully replying, "Would that be an iPhone 4 or an iPhone5?"' This was met by more laughter and resounding cheers.

Feeling buoyed up, I started entering competitions, including a masochistic night called 'The Blackout'. (Three audience members are given a 'blackout card', which they must hold up as soon as they deem you unfunny. Once all three cards are up, the lights plunge on stage and everyone boos you off. Such larks.) And although my jokes would sometimes fall as flat as a turd dropped from a balcony, those stand-up shows slowly gave me back a bit of the confidence that I had lost; the belief in myself that drama school had gradually stripped away.

Case in point: at the end of the three years' training, we were each called in for a meeting with the head of acting, who would advise us on our 'casting type' – the roles that we would most likely be auditioning for once out in the industry. One by one my year group went in and came out smiling.

'I've been told I'll be cast as the exotic seductress!' Alice announced, flicking back her glossy mane of hair.

'I'm apparently an English rose,' Robyn smiled. 'Most likely to be put up for roles in period dramas.'

Then it was my turn.

'Now then, Gabrielle,' the head of acting began, looking me up and down. 'As you are a rather a voluptuous girl, you fall into larger casting.' (For a brief moment I took this to mean bigger roles, such as West End leads or Hollywood blockbusters. I soon realised my mistake.) 'I see you playing something such as . . . the jolly nurse!'

The jolly nurse. The JOLLY FUCKING NURSE. (Ironically, my first professional role actually did turn out to be that of a fat, jolly nurse, but more on that later.)

Our graduation day fell in July. As I was in the process of moving flats, I thought I'd treat myself to a hotel the night before the ceremony – a beautiful room with a four-poster bed, booked online and ludicrously cut-price. Having checked in at 4 p.m. and realised that I had eighteen hours to kill before the dreaded event, I decided to pop along to M&S and buy myself a selection of nibbles and a few cans of ready-mixed cocktails, to be drunk in the luxury and seclusion of my private balcony. Four hours later and I am three sheets to the wind.

'GOOD EVENING!' I called down to a passer-by on the street below, cheerfully waving my fag and taking a slug of Harvey Wallbanger. She looked up, startled and horrified, before hurrying on past.

I awoke the following morning with a hangover strong enough to wake the dead. The sinking realisation that my drinking had extended beyond my modest few cans of cocktail was confirmed by a huge empty Prosecco bottle next to my bed, complete with an ice bucket and two glasses. (Why oh WHY did I ask for two glasses?! I have a horrible feeling that I filled them both up and 'cheersed' myself.)

Clearly a little peckish after my drunken guzzling, I also appeared to have ordered myself a room-service fish pie – an interesting choice for me, as normally my alcohol-fuelled food preferences lean towards anything coated in three pounds of cheese and lard.

Painfully aware that I needed to be in Chiswick in less than an hour to join my smiling, well-groomed classmates, I hurled myself into the shower, rapidly washed my hair and then stumbled around looking for my clothes. As my wet hair formed a dripping and tangled bird's nest on my head, I realised in horror that I had forgotten to pack a hair-brush. I am ashamed to admit that due to a combination of severe hangover, low self-esteem and general dread of the day before me, I resorted to brushing my hair WITH A FORK. A fork that had been sitting in the remnants of last night's fish pie.

The graduation ceremony itself was something of a gigantic anticlimax. Rather than feeling excitement and pride over what we had achieved, Katie and I sat on the wall behind the school, chain-smoking in our hats and gowns, passionately relieved that it was all over and we would never have to see the rest of our year group, or embody a piece of bamboo, ever again.

Even my parents, who had travelled all the way up from Wales, were a trifle disappointed by the day.

'Is that your head of year?' my mum whispered to me, dressed up to the nines in her best frock and hat. 'He looks a little ... SCRUFFY, doesn't he? Hasn't even bothered to put a tie on. He sat through that whole ceremony slouched in his chair with a face like a smacked bottom.'

After graduation, I ended up living with an old school friend named Rachel, who had finished a psychology degree at Bristol Uni and was now determined to come to London and experience the high life.

'Move in with me!' I cried in delight that summer, while temporarily living back home. 'I'm sick to death of west London. Let's go east and find ourselves a cheap little two-bed. Or a three-bed, and turn the third bedroom into a gym room. Or a GIN ROOM!'

It didn't quite go to plan. Having eventually found a very small two-bedroom flat in Canary Wharf (why we chose to live in the most boring, businessy part of London, I will never know), Rachel unexpectedly landed a job working for the London Fire Brigade.

I was beside myself at the thought of my flatmate shimmying down a fireman's pole, and hysterically excited by the assortment of burly men she would surely be bringing home – until she dropped the bombshell that she would actually be working for the Fire Safety Department. A nine-to-five office job with absolutely zero contact with any actual firemen.

In contrast to Rachel's stable routine and adult responsibilities, my life started to unravel dramatically into a year-long bender. I had landed absolutely no auditions since graduation and was working in an assortment of soulless part-time jobs, so naturally I filled my free time drinking heavily and frequenting the clubs of Soho.

I would come crashing in at all hours, often with a man in tow, doing over-the-top 'creeping', and repeating 'DON'T WAKE RACHEL UP!' in a stage whisper louder than a foghorn. Things reached a head one night when, having been kept up for nearly an hour by me crashing around in the dark, she heard me cry through the wall, 'MY GOD, YOUR COCK IS NEARLY AS TALL AS YOU ARE!'

It was at that point that I made the decision to stop ruining Rachel's life and move out. Having concluded that it would be better to live with complete strangers rather than destroy any more friendships, I ran a very specific search on a spare rooms website, detailing that I wanted to live with males only, in a smoking household that allowed pets. (I reasoned that if they were happy to share with animals, then they could most likely cope with me.)

Amazingly, an option came up for a dingy flat in Shepherd's Bush, sharing with two blokes who smoke and drink till the cows come home. Relieved, I moved in and have been living here in a disgusting state ever since.

And now Emma is engaged.

I stare at my flushed, tear-stained reflection in the mirror and experience a rare and startling moment of lucidity.

'Enough is enough,' I say aloud to myself, pulling back my shoulders and flicking a bit of egg off my T-shirt. 'I need to get it the FUCK together.'

I am determined not to turn up to Emma's wedding in a year's time in the same single, jobless and gin-riddled state. I refuse to hear the gleeful whispers of my friends' parents as they mutter, 'Such a shame, isn't it – all that potential gone to waste. That's London for you.' Or 'TERRIBLY RUDE. I offered her a glass of orange juice and she called me an old bint.'

No.

Come hell or high water, I am going to spend the next twelve months getting my shit together. This includes rebooting my failing acting career and finding myself a boyfriend in time for the wedding; one who is attractive, friendly and doesn't possess any weird fetishes, such as having sex with roller coasters or being aroused by teddy bears.

Feeling mad with euphoria, I splash gin into a glass and light another fag.

First things first: I need to get out of London and clear my head for a bit. NOT back home to Wales, where I will no doubt be engulfed in a tidal wave of bridal magazines, engagement ring flashes and worried looks from my parents. No. What I need, what I really and truly need . . . is a holiday.

I reach for my phone.

3

Amstersham

My love of red wine is no secret; in fact it's a staple element of my daily diet. I'm pretty sure that instead of blood, five litres of Merlot is pumping round my body.

So when, after graduating from drama school, I landed a job as a part-time adviser at an exclusive wine club, many people assumed that all my dreams had finally come true. The title 'wine adviser' was extremely deceptive, however. I was realistic in my expectations. It's not like I thought I'd be walking into a cosy firelit living room where four pipe-smoking men would be discussing the merits of a bottle of 1995 Chateau Margaux while some lithe young stripper named Chantelle gyrated in the background.

But I had expected the job to involve a *little* drinking. A few snifters here and there and a couple of surplus bottles of wine to take home each week.

Instead, on my first day I was led into a soulless call centre filled with about a hundred people, sat in front of a computer and given an on-screen script to use to flog cases of questionable-quality wine to randomly dialled numbers. Any consumption of alcohol was expressly forbidden.

As it turned out, I completely lacked gumption as a saleswoman. I should have guessed this, having spent twenty-three years completely lacking gumption as a customer. Excluding pubs and clubs, where my rather showboaty drunken alter ego will happily drape herself across the bar and harass the staff for a free shot of tequila, I otherwise possess an extremely British fear of making a fuss in any form of customer service situation. This has led to me quietly accepting wrong plates of food in restaurants, paying full price for items of clothing with half the buttons missing and a large smear of someone else's foundation round the collar, and not correcting the barista at my local Starbucks who has, rather worryingly, written my name as 'Gavin' on every single coffee order for the past six weeks.

So a job in which I earned commission for every crate of wine sold and had my calls listened in on by the floor manager was never going to end well.

It wasn't *entirely* my fault. I seemed to have a God-given gift for attracting the most rambling, maddest of loons to my call list. Here is how a regular conversation might go:

CUSTOMER: Hello?

ME: Hello, Mr Reynolds! It's Gabrielle here calling from Explorer Wine Club. How are you today?

CUSTOMER: [heavy sigh, followed by sound of chair being kicked out of the way and *Homes Under the Hammer* turned down in the background] WHO?

ME: Gabrielle! From Explorer Wine Club. We have some fantastic exclusive offers at the moment on a selection of red, white and sparkling cases. I'm sure you wouldn't want to miss out on them!

CUSTOMER: Don't need no wine.

ME: [hastily flicking through the script and forcing a hearty laugh] I appreciate what you're saying! But once you hear about the EXCLUSIVE HUGE DISCOUNTS on offer, I think you might change your mind.

CUSTOMER: Don't need no wine. Just had a colostomy bag installed.

ME: So! We have our Rustic Red Range, which includes . . . Sorry, what was that?

CUSTOMER: Colostomy bag.

ME: Oh, right. Gosh. Well, I quite understand. No wine

for you then! HAR HAR HAR! Well, sorry to have
kept you, have a lovely—

CUSTOMER: It's my bowel, see. The large one. Had what
the doctor called an intestinal obstruction.

[Sound of my floor manager clicking in to listen to
conversation]

ME: Oh dear, that does sound nasty. Well, I really
must be going, Mr Reynolds, I do hope you feel
better soon and—

CUSTOMER: A complete blockage, it was. I had these
awful stomach cramps, see. I said to Rita – that's my
wife – something's not right here, Rita love. And she
swore blind it will have been the Mexican beans we
had for dinner, as they've always made me a bit gassy
in the past—

ME: [slightly hysterical] Okay, well . . .

CUSTOMER: But then I had a full rectal examination and
handed in my stool sample—

ME: Bye! [hanging up]

I would then receive an almighty bollocking from my
furious manager, saying that my call time and sales ratio
were simply not good enough. I quite reasonably argued that
this was a stark improvement on my first approach to wine
selling, which went:

ME: Hello, Mrs Price! This is Gabrielle calling from
Explorer Wine Club.

CUSTOMER: I don't want any wine.

ME: Okay, not to worry, byeee! [hangs up]

The only bright spot in this acute misery was the two new friends I made, Danny and Rosie. Having been paired up on our first day, I immediately found a soulmate in Rosie, who was staring round at the dozens of computer screens with a horror parallel to my own.

We cheered up, however, when introduced to Danny, who would be training us up to use the phones.

'Phwoar, he's a bit of all right,' I said under my breath to Rosie as we were led over to his desk. Danny turned out to be not only a bit of all right, but an absolute hoot. In fact he would have quite possibly been my dream man were he not as gay as a daffodil and utterly fabulous with it.

Having already worked at the call centre for three months, Danny had developed a suitable loathing for the job and imparted to us some sage advice.

'Girls,' he said, lowering his voice and glancing around furtively, 'listen up and listen good. The only way to survive here is to DRINK THROUGH IT.'

Rosie and I took his advice very seriously.

We quickly realised that due to the huge number of people working in the call centre, we could actually sign out on the system, push off to the local pub for a couple of hours, sign back in again and carry on working. Seeing as we wouldn't actually be paid for the hours we were signed out for, we saw nothing wrong with this and congratulated ourselves on having found a way to survive the torturous ten-hour days.

It was just unfortunate that one Wednesday afternoon, while halfway through a bottle of Merlot, we were caught by our manager and swiftly fired.

'You can't fire us!' Rosie cried in outrage, valiantly trying to claw her way out of the situation. 'We are wine advisers. Our job, first and foremost, is to sample various wines and expand our palates. That bottle of Merlot was a form of vital research in order for us to deliver our best knowledge and opinions to our customers.'

Unsurprisingly, we were shown the door.

Danny was suitably horrified.

'But you told us we should drink!' I wailed to him as we stood having a final cigarette outside the building.

'Yes … I meant like decanting a gin and tonic into a Sprite bottle to sip at your desk, not going DOWN THE BLOODY PUB.'

So when I decide that what I desperately need is a holiday, it is Rosie – a kindred spirit if ever I've met one – that I call.

'I need to get out, Rosie,' I declare, pacing the room dramatically. 'Out of the country.'

'Okay, no problem,' she says in a deliberately calm voice. 'Tell me what you've done. Are the police involved?'

'No, nothing like that. I'm not on the bloody run!' I cry.

I briefly explain the whole Emma engagement scenario and my wish to have one final hurrah before I sort my life out.

'I see,' she replies, appreciating the gravitas of the situation immediately. 'Count me in. Where are we going?' God, I love her.

'I'm thinking sex shows. I'm thinking strapping young Dutchmen wearing clogs and clutching bongs.'

'Soho?'

'No, Amsterdam!'

And so the following Thursday, Rosie and I find ourselves at Heathrow Airport.

As it is only 8 a.m. and our flight doesn't leave for two hours, we make our way at a leisurely pace to one of the restaurants for a full English breakfast. We decide that our holiday has technically already started, and as it is noon somewhere in the world, as the old adage goes, we wash down our breakfast with two very strong Bloody Marys. Then, with a sigh of contentment, I sit back in my plastic chair and relax, feeling the delicious alcohol working its magic on my insides, blotting out the pain and turmoil of the past few days.

In a leisurely fashion I turn my gaze to the overhead TV screen, which is playing some sort of sports highlights programme.

'Do you know,' I muse to Rosie, 'I find football almost tolerable with the sound turned off. Sitting back with a cold drink, quietly perving on those strong thighs straining against those tight little shorts. Without all the whooping and yelling and having to pretend that I have a bloody clue about what's going on.

'IN FACT,' I continue, warming to my theme, 'I think they

should hold matches for a female-only audience, in which the men run around the pitch a bit and then proceed to STRIP, with their—'

With a jerk of horror, I suddenly notice the time displayed in the corner of the screen.

'Our flight leaves in half an hour!' I cry, and we grab our bags and charge out of the restaurant, tomato juice, vodka and cheap sausage meat churning violently around in our stomachs. We reach security in the unattractive state of 'drunkenly out of breath' and are met by one of those creepy robotic machines that scan your passport and face. Neither of us can get through.

'Oh, fuck it. Excuse me, sir!' I call, catching sight of a security man. 'KIND SIR! Yes, hello. Unfortunately your machine doesn't appear to be working, which is a bit of a sticky wicket as we are running a little late for our flight. Could you be a darling and let us through?'

The security man takes my boarding pass, then gives me a look somewhere between withering and murderous.

'You're in the wrong building, madam,' he replies. 'Your flight leaves from the North Terminal.'

If there is one distinct moment in my life when I've seriously feared for my levels of health and fitness, it is that run from the South to the North Terminal.

'Do you have any liquids?' wheezes an equally nauseous-looking Rosie when we eventually arrive.

'Only my antibacterial hand gel,' I reply, sending my bag through on the conveyor. 'We'll be on that plane in a jiffy.'

I am pulled over by three members of security almost immediately.

'Excuse me, madam. We need to look through your bag for any liquids or dangerous items,' states a stern-faced security guard. Her mouth is set in a thin straight line, reminding me unaccountably of Zippy from *Rainbow*.

'I don't have anything in there, I promise.' I smile at her, thinking that she must be new to the job and not have a clue what she's doing. 'But you can have a look anyway.'

She starts unzipping my bag.

'I learned to pack light, you see,' I say, nudging her playfully and earning a death stare in return. 'I was in the Brownies.'

What follows is mortifying.

One by one she pulls out every item in my bag, including bottles of shampoo and conditioner, shower gel, hair oil, suntan cream, a gigantic razor, nail scissors, my extremely large emergency 'period knickers' ('They're not mine, I promise!') and a row of AA batteries that look rather like bullets.

She gives me a very thorough ticking-off and all the 'offending items' are taken away to be destroyed, but finally we are allowed to board the plane. We then sit on the runway, delayed in the boiling heat, for about an hour and a half.

I would not by any means call myself a confident flyer, but my fear is nothing compared to Rosie's. She is a jibbering, jabbering mess. Having poured my bottle of Evian over her sweating face and shouted, 'FOR THE LOVE OF GOD, WHERE IS THE WINE TROLLEY?!' I decide that perhaps attempting to be a calming influence is a better tack.

'Ah, look, Rosie, we're setting off!' I say in a deliberately peaceful, everything-is-tickety-boo voice as the plane moves slowly away.

'Here we go along the runway ... just gaining a bit of speed now,' I intone as we racket along at about a hundred miles an hour.

'And here we are – up in the air!' I coo as the plane rises violently into the sky ... before casually dropping about forty feet.

'HOLY FUCKING SHIT!' I scream, any notion of being the calm one now completely abandoned. 'We can't die ... I haven't shaved!'

Rosie sits frozen and clammy-looking in her seat, like a half-finished Madame Tussaud's project.

I don't know what the pilot is on, but I can only liken the journey to the Dumbo the Flying Elephant ride at Disneyland. (For those of you who have not experienced the Dumbo the Flying Elephant ride at Disneyland, I only have one piece of advice – NEVER CHOOSE THE PINK ELEPHANT. It is by far the most overused and therefore unstable carriage, prone to jerking and dropping at any given minute. I will never forget my father's screams as we hurtled along to jubilant circus music.) At one point, we fly completely vertically for what feels like ten minutes.

The stag do behind us are, of course, loving it.

'Look, I can see the stars, lads!'

'You've always wanted to be an astronaut, Jim! HA HA HA.'

When we finally touch down in Amsterdam, Rosie and I

are traumatised and shaking. We cling to each other as we stagger down the plane's steps and make our way unsteadily across the vast runway to collect our bags.

Airport bag collection is always a nightmare. No matter what size case I bring, and however distinctive I try to make it (e.g. tying bows to the handle and sticking sparkly pom-poms across the front), mine is always the last to appear and is usually in some form of disarray. Once, on a family holiday to Florida, my case had clearly been run over by some sort of truck during transit. It finally arrived, crushed and duct-taped together, trailing T-shirts and underwear that I then had to chase round the conveyor belt.

This time, by a stroke of luck, both of our cases arrive intact, and we are soon outside the airport and boarding the tram (not, as I had imagined, an old wooden carriage pulled by a shire horse, but instead a disappointingly modern contraption; more like a large sliding bus) to our Airbnb flat, situated about half an hour from the city centre. We are greeted at the door by our host, a friendly-looking young man named Enrico.

'Hello, Enrico!' I smile, stepping inside. 'My name's Gabrielle and this is—'

'Are you scared of dogs?' he interrupts. 'Because I have a large German shepherd who doesn't like strangers. You don't want him jumping up at you in the night, he weighs forty-five kilos.'

Oh good.

Enrico teaches us some code words to use in case of any run-ins with the dog, and we head up to our room.

'OH MY GOD,' cries Rosie as soon as we're safely inside. 'I'm so sorry. It didn't mention anything about vicious hounds on the website! Just that there was free Wi-Fi and breakfast facilities!'

'Don't worry,' I reply. 'Let's just get out of here.'

We hastily change into our slutty evening attire.

'Oh shit.' Rosie looks down at herself as we head out the front door, trying to avoid a second run-in with Enrico. 'My nipples totally show through in this top. Oh well, I'm desperate.'

We get the tram straight to the red-light district.

I've heard much about Amsterdam's red-light district over the years. In my head, I have painted a rather fanciful picture of scantily clad women posing in windows, signs pointing towards live sex shows and people scattered around smoking bongs. As we step off the tram, I am amazed to discover that my predictions were not fanciful but instead bang on the money.

'Come on,' says Rosie, grabbing me by the arm as I gawp at a prostitute tickling her bum with a feather duster. 'We're going to get some magic mushrooms.'

I have never taken mushrooms before, but secretly imagine them to be a load of Mickey Mouse claptrap nonsense. A sort of herbal remedy thing like St John's Wort or Radox bubble bath. But not wanting to disappoint Rosie and be a party pooper, I decide to go along with it. Rosie, who has taken shrooms before, advises that we have a whole pack of the strongest variety each ('You have the tolerance of an ox,

Gabs'). She also warns me that they taste absolutely disgusting. Sitting in a bar, with two large gin and tonics in front of us, we crack them open.

'Good God, they're delicious!' I cry, casually eating them by the handful. 'So light! SO WOODY! I could take these with me as a snack to the gym!'

While we wait for them to start working, we start looking around for unsuspecting men to pull. But an hour later, my suspicions are confirmed – the shrooms have no effect on us whatsoever.

'We must just be immune to them, Rosie,' I say, putting a consoling arm around her and draining my glass. 'I did eat a lot of mushroom risotto as a child.'

Despondently we head to another bar.

Suddenly I find that I cannot stop laughing. The smallest thing is outrageously funny and I am crying and drooling in an effort to explain what I am laughing about. 'That light . . . It's . . . It's . . . IT'S SHAPED LIKE A COCK!'

And then Rosie finds she is doing the same.

Then the hallucinations begin. Oh God, the hallucinations.

There is a lot of the night I don't remember, but I can tell you very clearly that every time I look at Rosie she has a unicorn's horn coming out of her forehead. And that whenever I glance at the spotty bow in her hair, it sets me off on a train of jungle-themed hallucinations. The spots on the bow will somehow morph into dancing leopards, and then everywhere I look everyone has got either a giraffe or a leopard's head. This sounds quite scary but I enjoy it immensely.

In fact, I find that if I focus on any object or word for too long, then I will see it *everywhere*.

'We need to find some gin, Rosie. Oh, actually, don't worry! That man's FACE is made of gin!'

Somehow we find our way to another bar, where we sit in a dark corner, deciding to just quietly ride the whole thing out. I glance at Rosie, noting with relief that the horn on her forehead has reduced to more of a blurry stump. Thank God, the hallucinations seem to be abating. It is at that moment that we are approached by a young couple.

'Hey!' says the girl. 'We overheard you guys chatting. Are you from England too?'

Well, that does it.

At the mention of the word 'England', my addled brain kicks back into hallucination mode, and the couple in front of me turn into a walking, talking map of the British Isles.

'Are you okay?' asks Cornwall.

'Excuse me,' I say to Norfolk, grabbing Rosie's arm and running outside.

We had planned on making loads of friends and meeting eligible young men, but instead Rosie and I spend the entire night walking through the streets linked tightly arm in arm – me wearing my gigantic sunglasses – both as fried as eggs.

We reach a particular low point at around 3 a.m., when Rosie becomes paranoid that everyone in the red-light district is talking about us (it is probably a fair assessment) and also, rather creepily, seems convinced that I am her mother.

I decide I need to take control of the situation.

'I've got this shit, Rosie!' I cry. 'Don't look me in the eye for five minutes. MOTHER NEEDS TO CONCENTRATE!'

I flag down a rickshaw.

'Hello, young man,' I begin, trying not to be put off by the fact that he has the head of a rabbit. 'We need to get out of here. Immediately. We also urgently need cash, cigarettes and kebabs.'

He cycles us out of the red-light district to a cashpoint (a blur of shapes and colours), where I see fit to withdraw three hundred euros – otherwise known as the entire contents of my account. 'We don't know how much we will need, Rosie,' I say. 'We don't know how much we will NEED!' The rickshaw driver then takes us to a kebab shop.

'Right. Here is the plan,' I say confidently. 'There is a very vicious dog at home and we need chips to throw him off the scent. When we get back, you will run upstairs while I distract him.'

We can hear the sounds of rabid barking as soon as we arrive at the house.

'RUBBER BALL!' I shout through the letter box. 'Shit, what were the code words? Friendly dog! Friend not foe! COCK!'

Eventually I resort to charging through the door ahead of Rosie and hurling my box of chips and gravy in the direction of the rather startled-looking dog (unfortunately missing and hitting the fridge), giving us enough time to charge up the stairs and collapse into our bedroom, panting and cross-eyed.

I awake the following afternoon with a crashing headache and complete disbelief at last night's events.

'How is it, Rosie, that I can drink an entire litre of gin and be absolutely fine, yet a few God-given mushrooms, VEGETABLES really, have the capability to send me completely off my rocker?'

We both agree that we should take it easy today, planning a late lunch, a spot of clothes-shopping and perhaps a couple of glasses of wine before bed.

We set off in the opposite direction from the red-light district, wandering down cobbled streets, soaking up the culture and keeping our eyes peeled for a restaurant. It is then that we come across a shop called When Nature Calls.

Under the mutual pretence of 'sticking our heads in', we find ourselves in the most extravagant X-rated store imaginable. Our lunch plans quickly go out the window.

Completely overwhelmed by the selection, we purchase: two pipes, a hash lolly, a packet of erotic gum and sex pills ('When in Amsterdam, Rosie!'), some laughing gas balloons, a box of space cookies and twenty more grams of magic mushrooms.

By the end of the afternoon, having washed down a spliff with our entire pack of cookies, we have reached the stage of 'fat, stoned and in the way'. We then head to a bar, deciding it is time for round two of the shrooms.

I think this says a lot about my hideously middle-class, daddy's-girl upbringing, but that night I become obsessed with Shetland ponies. To the point where, sitting on the toilet, I AM a Shetland pony.

A very sassy, chubby little Shetland pony.

'Where's my hoof oil?' I call out to Rosie in the next cubicle, only half-joking. 'THIS BITCH NEEDS HOOF OIL!'

The bell for last orders rings in the bar.

'That will be my call for the gymkhana!' I cry, galloping out of the toilet, whinnying.

Hiccuping and crying with laughter, we then decide that now would be an excellent time to try the erotic gum and sex pills. Rosie goes first.

'Quickly, take yours!' she shouts. 'I'm soon to become very horny!'

I don't know whether it is the gum or the pills, but something has a rather alarming effect on me. Neither of us could feel less horny if we tried, but I become convinced that every man in Amsterdam is hitting on me. And I am not happy about it.

'Oh God, look at that man brazenly winking at me,' I mutter in disgust. 'Look away, you perv! Stop undressing me with your eyes!'

The night ends with me starting a fight with some poor man in Burger King who I swear is trying to pinch my arse, and when we eventually get back to the flat, Rosie projectile-vomits into her Burger King bag, which then disintegrates on to the carpet.

We don't speak of the Shetland pony/sex pills incident the following morning. It is the elephant in the room. The horse in the room. Instead we pack our bags, post our keys back through the letter box (probably to be swiftly eaten by the dog) and head off for our much-talked-about but never achieved lunch.

'So, Gabs,' begins Rosie as we sit at opposite ends of a table groaning under the weight of an inordinate amount of chips, pizza and pasta. 'How are you feeling about everything now? Ready to go back?'

The thought of what awaits me at home – the build-up to Emma's wedding, along with my resolve to find a stable boyfriend and generally get my life together – slaps me in the face like a wet lettuce.

'Well, it hasn't QUITE been the relaxing break I had planned. You know, what with the weed and the sex pills and the ten hours spent as a horse. But yep. Ready for London.' I stuff three chips into my mouth. 'Can we fit in a tourist attraction before we leave?'

Have you ever found that when you're dreading something, you can discover joy in the most mundane of tasks that will delay it that little bit longer? Like needing to leave for work but suddenly getting immeasurable pleasure from bleaching the toilet or plucking out your ingrown hairs. Well, keen to postpone our trip to the airport for as long as possible, we find ourselves unexpectedly having the time of our lives at the cheese museum.

'Look, Rosie! The journey of the Vintage Gouda. Fascinating!' I exclaim, intently reading a mind-numbingly dull placard on the wall about milk curdling and lactic acid. 'Apparently it's the brine solution that gives the cheese its nutty and distinctive taste. Who knew?'

Rosie meanwhile is being helped into a traditional Dutch

farmer's costume by a member of staff, to have her photo taken with a wheel of Edam.

After stuffing ourselves with free samples and paying a visit to the gift shop, we head reluctantly to the airport, Rosie carrying her heavy bag of sick-covered clothes and me my recently purchased Old Goat. (The cheese, that is, not some billy goat with a bell round its neck. Although to be honest, a simple life of curdling cheese and rearing goats is starting to look more appealing.)

For the entire plane ride home I am aware of a gnawing sense of dread in my stomach. A premonition, if you will. I shake it off, telling myself it's simply the end-of-holiday blues. Like Sunday nights as a child, when I had a whole Biff and Chip book to read, my times tables to learn and a week of school ahead of me.

No, there's absolutely nothing to be fearful about. Things are going to be great back in London. Spiffing, in fact! Quite frankly, I struggle to see how they could get any worse. (Unless another friend gets engaged, I burn the flat down, or my mother announces that she's leaving my father to have an affair with the milkman.)

As they say, the only way is up.

I turn to Rosie.

'As we're technically still on holiday, shall we have a few more Bloody Marys at Heathrow?'

4

Back to Reality

In the absence of any actual paid acting jobs, I am currently working in a restaurant called The Scoff in east London. It is a hideously hipster establishment, serving the most pretentious food and drink known to humankind.

Drinks include a 'White Peach and Gin Fizz' (why you

would choose to cheapen such a beautiful, sophisticated spirit in such a manner is beyond me. A bit like dressing the Queen up in a pair of suspenders and a tickle feather and making her perform the Cha Cha Slide) and a 'Carrot Beet Shrub', which frankly sounds like something my father would grow in his manure patch, but is apparently some sort of trendy alcoholic vegetable beverage.

The food is on a similar ego trip. A simple spaghetti bolognaise becomes a 'Deconstructed Spaghetti Bolognaise', where diners are faced with the hilariously fun task of mixing the pasta, sauce and cheese together themselves, at the table, OUT OF JARS; while the good old-fashioned fish and chips comes with the fish, in goujon form, strung from a MINI WASHING LINE and the chips beneath it in a teeny-tiny hamster-sized trolley.

The decor is even worse. I *think* the look they were going for was 'edgy urban eatery', but it has actually ended up as 'school dinner hall'.

The first challenge upon entering (having been lured in by the oh-so-hilarious and Instagram-ready sign outside saying 'Fat people are harder to kidnap. Stay safe and eat lots here!' HA HA HA!) is finding your way through the dark to your seat. The whole place is lit by just ten bare light bulbs dangling from exposed wires. How a place charging £14 for a plate of sausage and mash can't afford a few nice lampshades, I do not know. But then what do I know about cutting-edge hipster fashion?

Having successfully made it to your seat without crashing

into a passing waiter or tripping over and smacking your head on the red tile floor, you may be surprised to find yourself sitting at a long wooden table along with ten complete strangers. A bit like your first day in the school canteen. It is also a bit of a Russian roulette as to which chair you will get to sit on. Half the fun here at The Scoff is that ALL THE CHAIRS ARE TOTALLY DIFFERENT AND DON'T MATCH ONE ANOTHER IN THE SLIGHTEST! The more fortunate customers may find themselves on the green squishy armchair or the high-backed wooden chair with the gold-tasselled cushion. If you're unlucky, though, you may end up on the rusted metal garden chair, or the stool, where you awkwardly find yourself about six inches higher than everyone else at the table, having to bend down to reach your plate.

When I interviewed for my job at The Scoff, I was determined that I wanted to work behind the bar. I'd worked as a waitress before and LIKE HELL was I doing it again. During my gap year, when the majority of my friends were travelling the world or starting at university, I took a job in a fish restaurant.

It was ghastly. Not only did the kitchen porters take great delight in locking me in the industrial-sized fridge every evening, but I was incapable of taking orders correctly, carrying piles of plates or clearing tables. One of the worst instances was when I dropped a plate of fishcakes from the top floor of the restaurant to the bottom, only to be skidded on by a passing customer on his way to the toilet.

No, the bar was where I belonged. The sticky, dirty bar.

The fact that I had never worked behind a bar before did not deter me. I was taken with images of myself cackling loudly with the locals, then singing an East End ditty before perhaps hitching my skirt up and performing a rousing dance routine to the amusement of the assembled punters. (It's possible that my idea of bar work may have been influenced by the film *Coyote Ugly* and the role of Nancy in *Oliver!*).

I had actually inadvertently ended up behind a bar in the past, in a nightspot called Wine Not in Cardiff. I'd drunkenly ordered a glass of rosé, only to be told by the gregarious owner, Antonio, that they didn't serve rosé, but I was welcome to come behind the bar and mix myself half a glass of red and half a glass of white and 'we see what de result is, chica!'.

I was interviewed for my job at The Scoff by the bar manager, who was called – wait for it – Waldo. Instead of strolling in wearing a red-and-white-striped jumper and hat, however, this Waldo greeted me wearing skinny jeans, a tucked-in shirt and a beanie. (Since getting to know him, I have come to suspect that Waldo is not his real name at all. I imagine him to have been christened something normal and mundane, like Jeff.)

I found 'Waldo' a deeply confusing character. Although he had a pinched, feral sort of face (he reminded me of Moley from *The Wind in the Willows*), his intense brown eyes suggested an air of authority that made me want to simultaneously impress him with my bar knowledge and take him home for a rigorous round of buggery.

'So, Gabby,' he began, glancing down my outrageously fabricated CV. 'You've had experience working in a bar before?'

'Oh yes.' I nodded. 'I used to work in a pub in Wales.'

He stared at me encouragingly. 'Called?'

'Called . . . called . . .' I surreptitiously glanced at a rather overweight lady waiting at the nearest bus stop. 'Called The Lardy Gypsy.'

'Right.' He frowned. 'And what sort of cocktails are you used to making?'

'Oh, hundreds.' I smiled reassuringly. 'Mojito . . . Gin and tonic . . . Dark 'n' Stormy.'

'Good, good.' He nodded. (GOD, those eyes were brown. I could drown in them. Like a dung beetle stuck in a pot of molasses.)

'Um . . . Sex on the Beach.'

'Excellent.' He smiled. (Wow, good strong teeth. A little wonky, but strong. Like Austin Powers.)

'And . . . um . . .'

'Yes?'

'SIT ON MY FACE.'

'Right.' He frowned. 'I've not heard of that one.'

'It's a Welsh speciality,' I assured him.

And so, through a series of bare-faced lies, I landed the job.

It started badly, with the uniform. I had several friends who worked in bars. The majority of them got to wear jeans and the company T-shirt (sexily slashed with a pair of scissors to flatter their figure), while the others were allowed to wear whatever the hell they wanted.

I was made to wear . . . TWEED. Actual *tweed*. On my first day on the job, I was presented with a tweed waistcoat and an ill-fitting pair of tweed trousers. I looked like a cross between Sherlock Holmes and a Fortnum & Mason luxury hamper.

'Right!' Waldo called to the team, loudly clapping his hands together. 'We have Gabby joining our team tonight!'

The mainly Polish bar crew glared at me in disgust.

'Now we're very lucky, because Gabby has a huge amount of experience working behind a bar in Wales. She's going to be teaching us a few things tonight, including a traditional Welsh cocktail called Sit on My Face!'

How I got through that first shift I will never know.

Watched beadily by Waldo, I started slamming together random concoctions of gin, sugar syrup and decomposed orange slices, all the while plastering a smile on my face and trying inconspicuously to tug free the camel toe caused by my tweed trousers. After several customers were rendered red-faced and choking by my inventions (who knew that gin, tequila and cinnamon schnapps is NOT a good mix?), Waldo took control of the situation, ordering me to just pull the pints and signing me up for unpaid out-of-hours cock-tail training.

The clientele at The Scoff are awful. We are talking cocaine-fuelled businessmen fresh from their stint at the stockbrokers', ready to sink overpriced pints and bray about how many millions they made that day. Yet somehow I have managed three months here without punching anyone, glugging gin straight from the bottle or being fired.

One week back from Amsterdam, and suffering from some sort of post-magic-mushroom crash, I am in no mood to be trifled with.

'Gabby?' Waldo calls. 'We're out of Amstel. Can you go and change the barrel?'

Oh God, please not the barrels. I had an intense training session with Waldo on my first day, in which he took me down to the basement and explained how to turn on the gas and change the various kegs. Unfortunately, instead of listening, I spent the entire half-hour convinced that this was all an elaborate ruse to seduce me, and therefore focused all my attention on trying to lean coquettishly over the barrels. (I also, shamefully, must admit that there was a moment when we were standing by some sort of air vent and I decided to position myself directly in front of it, allowing my hair to billow out behind me in what I hoped looked like Beyoncé in the midst of a music video, but in actual fact probably looked more like Edward Scissorhands in the midst of a blizzard.)

'Gabby ... THE AMSTEL!' Waldo screams, waving his hand in front of my vacant face.

'Right, yes, no problem!' I chirp. 'Off to change the barrel I go!'

Luckily I am saved at that moment by a gaggle of suited men heading to the bar.

'All right, sweetheart?' one of them asks, squeezing his arse cheeks on to a ludicrously high bar stool.

I stare stonily back.

'How's your day going then?'

Oh, it's going just *great*. I've cleaned a two-week-old lemon from behind the fridge, dropped a large box of tonic waters on my foot and am hoping to swing by Boots tonight in order to pick up some cream for the fresh bout of thrush caused by my tweed trousers.

'Sublime, thank you.' I smile icily.

Having served the wanker his pint – coating my hands and arms in a sticky layer of froth (every single pint I pour ends up being a quarter liquid and three quarters froth, leading to an exhausting and humiliating charade of pouring and tipping while the drip trays slowly fill to the brim and start over-flowing on to my shoes) – I escape to the luxury of the staff toilet.

I say 'luxury' . . . the staff toilet is actually about as opulent as the Chokey in *Matilda* – a tiny room filled with boxes of serviettes, buckets of bleach and a variety of mops sticking out at dangerous angles.

But to me it is a blessed excuse to sit down for five minutes and escape the hell of the bar.

As with every loo break, I pull out and check my phone.

I am greeted by a Facebook notification telling me I've been added to the group 'Bridesmaids!!!'

I open it with a sickening feeling of dread.

Hey girlies! ☺ ☺ ☺ *Natasha here, maid of honour.*

'Deep, calming breaths, Gabrielle,' I whisper, forcing myself to read on.

*Sooo Em's wedding is approaching, which means one thing . . .
HEN DO PLANNING!!! Basically, I've divided Em's friends into
two groups – her really close ones (us!) and her not so close friends,
like work people, etc.*

Oh this is just bloody typical, I think to myself. Here she
goes already, assembling a group of people she's never met
into some sick friendship hierarchy, with herself at the top
and the plebeians down the bottom.

*So we're going to have a night out in Cardiff, which everyone's
invited to (and us girls will stay in The Bay Spa Hotel and have a
spa day), then for the second hen, us bridesmaids will surprise Ems
and go abroad . . . I'm thinking Ibiza? I thought it would be super-
cool to make it a REAL surprise and all chip in to pay for Em's plane
ticket. Let me know your thoughts. EXCITED!! <3 <3*

I am momentarily stupefied. A second hen do . . . to IBIZA?
Who does she think we are, the Pussycat Dolls?

My job at The Scoff pays the minimum wage of £6.70 per
hour. Every penny I earn is carefully counted and saved in
order to afford to live in this cramped, smelly, overpriced
city. I am sure that my friends at home imagine my life in
London to be an endless roller coaster of cocktail parties,
fancy dinners and trips to Harrods. In actual fact, I travel
everywhere by bus, shop at Primark and recently hunted
down my nearest Lidl.

(Note: my trip to Lidl turned out to be a COMPLETE
disaster. I have an ancient car in London, which I've driven
since I was seventeen and which stays resolutely parked on
the road outside my flat. Desperately needing to do a food

shop and deciding to economise, I took it on a rare outing, driving the six miles to Lidl. Having filled up a trolley with food, for the astounding price of £24, and queued for about an hour at the till, I drove home feeling very pleased with myself. A week later I received a letter through the post. Inside were black-and-white *Crimewatch*-style photos of me behind the wheel, entering and exiting the car park. The letter stated that I had exceeded my parking time limit and therefore must pay a NINETY-POUND FINE. Making my frugal little jaunt the most bloody expensive shopping trip I have ever made. I am sticking with Tesco.)

It's all right for Natasha. She still lives at home, where she runs a bafflingly successful business from the comfort of her parents' house. She must be haemorrhaging money.

I know that I should step in here and be the voice of reason. From the comfort of my poo-stained staff loo I should fire a quick message back suggesting that not everyone will be able to afford such an extravagant trip and that we should instead pre-drink a few bottles of Echo Falls and stick to a cheap and cheerful night in town.

But the old, childish, competitive side of me stops me. I can't let Natasha win. I can't let her jet off to Ibiza and her luxury spa day without me. I can't stomach the Facebook statuses, Instagram photos and yet another hint that she's closer to Emma than I will ever be.

FABULOUS IDEA, NAT, COUNT ME IN. HURRAH, CAN'T WAIT!!! I type back, worrying immediately that I've perhaps over-egged the pudding.

Feeling slightly light-headed, I open up the next horror lurking on my phone: an email from my agent, Steve.

Allow me to fill you in.

Since graduating a year ago, I have received absolutely no acting work. I realise that this is partly my own fault, and 'a bad craftsman blames his tools' and all that. But this has not been helped by my agent putting me up for the most ludicrous and inappropriate auditions known to humankind.

Such auditions include:

- An STI information video in which I had to 'dress for a night out in Watford' and be chased around the room by imaginary sexual diseases.
- A short film in which I auditioned for the character of an 'older and more overweight version of Vicky Pollard'. (I am embarrassed to admit that the casting director actually selected me for this audition. As in, he will have scanned through a database of hundreds of faces, stopped at mine and gone, 'FUCK ME, SHE'S A RIGHT MUNTER!' and called me in.)
- The role of a magician's assistant. This, initially, sounded rather glamorous and exciting. Perhaps I was to be the next Debbie McGee! Until I realised I was actually auditioning for the role of a magician's assistant in an advert for a Norwegian sewage company.

My most recent, most humiliating casting occurred several weeks ago. My agent had sent me to an audition for a household cleaning brand that required no script. As soon as I turned up to the casting room, it was clear that something was amiss. Sitting before me were about twelve middle-aged black women.

The casting director came out and stared at me.

'Sorry ... which role were you here to audition for?' she asked.

'The wife,' I replied, feeling all eyes in the room on me.

'Oh, right. Well, the role is actually for a non-Caucasian woman in her thirties to forties.'

Great.

So in order to support myself financially in London and avoid moving back home, where I am without exception treated as a six-year-old (I recently excused myself from the dinner table to go to the toilet, only to be asked by my father: 'Is it big jobs?'), I have undertaken a variety of 'flexible' posts. Flexible in the sense that if necessary I could chop and change my shifts to fit around auditions. Ironically, the auditions have been so few and far between that I could quite frankly have taken up a full-time position as a school teacher and never once had to take a day off. Anyway.

Apart from the hell of being a wine adviser, without a doubt my worst job to date was for the Waggy Dog Company. I love dogs. I have grown up with them and they are as much a part of our family as my aunts, uncles and cousins. (Actually, much more a part of our family due to the fact that we barely speak to my aunts, uncles and cousins, but that is a whole other story.)

Dogs don't care what you look like or how popular you are. To them, you are at your most beautiful wearing no make-up, in your slightly ripe-smelling Tweety Pie pyjamas and crying into a tub of Ben & Jerry's because you haven't been invited to a sixth-form party. (Although, to be honest, at that age I couldn't really give a stuff about parties and was more likely to be crying about the fact that I hadn't got the lead role in the school production of *Jekyll and Hyde* and had instead been cast as Whore Number One.)

When I moved to London, one of the things I really missed was being around dogs. I would enviously watch owners throwing sticks for their spaniels in Chiswick Park, or find myself drunkenly running across the road on a night out to tearfully hug a passing boxer. (By boxer, I mean the breed of dog. Not Mike Tyson. Or a pair of men's briefs.)

Then I hit a brainwave. Why not work as a part-time dog-walker? It would be perfect! Fresh air, exercise and the chance to walk, hug and play with my canine friends. God, west London was teeming with rich housewives – they must all have pedigree dogs shut away and in need of my services!

I created an ad on Gumtree, with a photo of me romping in a field with our Labrador Archie. This led to me receiving a number of phone calls, none of them relating to dog-walking. I quickly abandoned the idea of freelancing and decided to Google some local companies instead. It was then that I came across a job advert with the Waggy Dog Company.

The advert was for a part-time position, requiring someone physically fit (I skated over this condition), happy with early-morning starts (skated over this too) and comfortable handling all breeds of dog. The candidate also needed to possess a full, clean driver's licence.

This last did strike me as quite odd, but I reassured myself that it must be for emergency purposes only. Perhaps in the event of a dog needing to be speedily driven to the vet's having twisted its ankle running after a ball, or chipped its tooth chewing on a particularly large stick.

I filled in my application form and received an invitation to attend a trial shift the next morning.

A VAN ARRIVED FOR ME AT 6 A.M.

Blazoned across the side, in big cartoonish writing, was the logo 'THE WAGGY DOG COMPANY'. Beneath this was a garish cartoon of three grinning dogs arm in arm, looking less waggy and more completely pissed, as if walking back from the pub together and about to burst into a rendition of 'I've Got a Lovely Bunch of Coconuts'.

An exhausted-looking young woman jumped out.

'You must be Gabrielle,' she said, shaking my hand. 'My name's Irina.'

'Hi, Irina.' I smiled, thoroughly bemused by the whole situation.

'I tell you what, it's going to be a relief handing this bugger over to you,' she said, gesturing to the van, which was already blocking a line of angry cars on my tiny residential road.

'That's ... for me?' I stuttered, staring in horror at the

ten-foot-long monster. 'But I don't have a licence for it!'

'A normal driver's licence will cover you for a vehicle this size,' she replied, opening the passenger door for me. 'Come on, we need to get moving.'

We proceeded to drive all over west London, collecting around fifteen dogs from their homes and putting them in the back of the van.

'Now these are very rich clients who don't wish to be disturbed by us in the morning,' Irina informed me. 'So when you go into the house, you have to do so SILENTLY. Just grab the dog, put his lead on and GO, locking the door behind you.'

Once we had collected our canine troupe, we drove to the day-care centre, where each dog received two walks and a meal before being dropped off home in the van.

Having spent the day in a silent state of shock, numbly following Irina around and occasionally crouching down to pick up a dog turd, I was wrongly assumed to be enjoying myself and offered the job. I was not in a position financially to refuse, so I found myself accepting.

'Right!' Irina said cheerily, as she dropped me home at about 8 p.m. 'You'll need to pick the van up from the centre at half past five tomorrow morning so that you can begin your rounds at six. Any problems, call the office, not me, as I won't be working here any more! Ha ha ha! Good luck!' And with that she gaily threw me the keys and drove off into the distance, blissful in the knowledge that some halfwit had foolishly agreed to take over her role.

My first day was a nightmare.

First things first. Those in possession of a car licence should NOT, without proper training, be allowed to drive a van. Especially someone like me.

'SHIT!' I screamed, as after stalling four times I finally got the van going again, only to nearly shoot straight across a busy junction.

Having taken off the wing mirrors of several passing cars and almost hit a number of pedestrians, I finally arrived at my first location. Ignoring the swearing of people trying to drive past me, I parked the van haphazardly in the middle of the road and let myself into the house.

I saw what Irina meant about rich clients. I found myself in a huge open-plan kitchen, pitch-black bar the light coming from the control panel of a huge double fridge.

'Dixie!' I whispered, swearing as I crashed into a stool and sent a load of papers flying on to the floor.

I heard a low growling in the corner.

'Come on, Dixie!' I whispered, turning on my iPhone torch and locating an angry-looking bichon frise sitting in a plush basket in the corner.

The little shit wouldn't move.

'It's okay, Dixie, I'm not an intruder,' I chattered nervously, reaching out tentatively to stroke him.

Eventually I resorted to dragging Dixie's basket all the way to the front door, then physically tipping him out on to the pavement. Once out of the house, he suddenly perked up, wagging his tail at me in a traitorous manner and hopping merrily into the van.

TWO HOURS later, I finally picked up my last dog and began the perilous drive to the day-care centre.

Now you would think that in order to transport that number of dogs, there would be some sort of cage system. Alas, no. All fifteen were allowed to roam freely around the back of the van. At one hideous moment, I pulled up at the traffic lights and three of the dogs CLIMBED OVER THE SEAT AND INTO THE FRONT WITH ME. I found myself staring into the eyes of a Jack Russell sitting on the dashboard.

I eventually arrived an hour late at the centre, sweating and shaking, and decided there and then that this was not the job for me.

Another job that will forever haunt my dreams was my brief stint as a children's party entertainer – a classic gig for out-of-work actors. It involved a training day where I would learn an assortment of skills, including magic tricks and balloon animals.

'Now then, girls,' said our manager, Tracie, 'we have a variety of costumes for you to wear. You'll take these home with you today on loan, and will be responsible for dry-cleaning them and bringing them with you to any engagements.'

One by one she surveyed us and started handing out outfits, including Queen Elsa from *Frozen* and Rapunzel.

She got to me.

'Hmm,' she said, looking me up and down. 'I think we'll try a different one for you.'

To my horror, she handed me a clown costume, complete

with a giant hula hoop to go inside the waistband of the trousers, and red braces to hold them up.

I stared at her, aghast.

'We have a lot of requests for clowns!' She smiled at me. 'We'll make sure that you're really confident making your balloon animals.'

Well. It soon became clear that I did NOT possess the natural flair for novelty balloon-making. I was given a pump and a packet of balloons to take home with me to practise, and I sat up for the next three nights desperately trying to get the hang of it via a series of online tutorials.

My friends were beside themselves with laughter.

'Try this one!' Robyn said, pointing to a picture of a balloon flower.

The problem was, every time I started inflating the balloon, it would somehow detach itself from the pump and whizz around the room like some large unruly condom.

I messaged the manager and begged her to give me some more time to practise, but in spite of my pleas, I was ruthlessly booked on my first job. Needless to say, it was a disaster from start to finish. After exploding a balloon in the faces of several crying children, I then moved on to my magic tricks.

'Look, everyone!' I cried, honking my red plastic nose to catch their attention. 'Fabby Gabby is going to do some magic for you all!' (I very much resented my clown name, due to it regularly being misheard as 'Flabby Gabby'.)

Shakily I drew out my magic colouring book from my bag.

'As you will see, all the pages are blank,' I began, in my most reverent and mystical of voices. 'But watch what happens when I use my magic wand!'

Now the secret behind the magic colouring book is to move your thumb into different positions before flipping through the book. This would hold back certain pages. Hold your thumb at the bottom and all the pages will be blank. Hold it at the top and black and white pictures will suddenly appear. Subtly slide your thumb to the middle and those pictures will magically become coloured in. If performed properly, this trick is a sure-fire crowd-pleaser.

'Who would like to be my special assistant?' I asked, looking pleadingly round at the children.

Eventually the birthday girl was reluctantly pushed forward by her mother.

'So, Bethany, all I need you to do is tap the book three times with the wand and then everyone shouts ABRACADABRA!'

Nervously she tapped the wand as a few children muttered the magic word.

'And now you will see that the white pages have magically formed pictures!' I cried, looking down at the book in triumph.

Shit. They were all still blank.

'Ah, sorry . . . HA HA HA! I forgot that the magic will only work if Fabby Gabby is wearing her magic coat!' I improvised wildly, grabbing a nearby leather jacket belonging to one of the parents. 'And again. ABRACADABRA!'

This time I dropped the book and swore under my breath,

at which point several children were hurried away by their parents.

Somehow I made it through the two hours, afterwards chain-smoking in my car (still in costume) and vowing that Fabby Gabby would never surface again.

SO. Desperate to get out of these humiliating dead-end jobs, I'd emailed my agent Steve several weeks ago, asking him if there were any auditions on the horizon.

Still sitting on the toilet, I click open his reply.

Hello Gabrielle, begins the email. *Sorry things have been a bit quiet of late. I'm going to be brutally honest with you – it's not looking good. Currently we are doing a lot of casting for panto season and the call this year seems to be for dwarves and women over the age of sixty. Will let you know if anything comes up. Steve x*

I fight the urge to angrily email back, *OH REALLY, STEVE?! It's strange, but I've been watching a lot of new BBC dramas and Channel 4 comedies recently, and funnily enough there seems to be A DISTINCT LACK OF DWARVES AND OAPS! Perhaps we should branch out our search a little?*

Instead, I send a feeble reply saying that it's all absolutely fine and I've got lots to be getting on with in the meantime. Just as I'm pulling up my trousers ready to head back to the bar (yes, I HAVE been sitting this whole time with them down around my ankles), my phone pings again.

Gabs!! says Emma on Facebook Messenger. *All the brides-maids are meeting up this Saturday night for dinner round mine. I know how busy you are in London, but would you have any time between acting jobs to pop down?*

I try not to burst into tears at my friend's ill-placed faith in my career.

Sure I can move a few things around, I type back, hating myself as I do so. *Count me in.*

Right. Better bloody book some time off work then.

5

Scurvy

Section A - Flowers
Class 1	Arrangement in a Wine Glass
Class 2	A Single Bloom
Class 3	A Posy of Garden Flowers

Section B – Vegetables
Class 1	6 Runner Beans
Class 2	1 Onion
Class 3	6 Tomatoes
Class 4	3 Courgettes
Class 5	3 Bunches of Herbs
Class 6	Selection of 5 Vegetables

Section C – Baking
Class 1	1 Victoria Sponge
Class 2	6 Welsh Cakes
Class 3	6 Biscuits

I really enjoy driving. The roar of the traffic, the blaring of horns, the abuse hurled by passing cyclists. It is a shame, therefore, that no one else seems to enjoy having me on the road.

It's not that I'm a *bad* driver. It's just that I possess a staggering lack of spatial awareness and coordination.

It is an affliction that has encumbered me from a young age. Physically unable to catch a ball, I was placed in the 'C' netball team at school. Being in the C team was social suicide – the 'pity squads' compiled of the most sportily inept students. Banned from playing matches against other schools, we spent our training sessions passing a foam ball to one another in a circle, while wearing yellow bibs that smelled like the collective BO of the entire post-pubescent male population of the school.

My ultimate fear, however, was reserved for maths class – a subject one wouldn't imagine required a great deal of coordination. For 'a bit of fun', our teacher would whip out a small sandbag (to the delighted whoops of my moronic classmates) and throw it to us one by one, while testing us on our times tables. I would studiously stare at my shoes, willing for the hell to be over, before inevitably being clocked on the head by the sandbag and having to scrabble around for it under my desk, like some overweight concussed Labrador.

I think the final straw came when, aged fifteen, I was deemed to have a flair for shot put. Taking in my robust build and Miss Trunchbull-like arms, my deluded PE teacher decided that finally she had found a sport I could excel at.

'No, no really,' I stammered as she passed me the seven-stone ball. 'I assure you, I may be strong but I have no aim.'

My protests fell on deaf ears and I found myself entered to represent my house at the school sports day. I hated sports day. I have an instant mistrust of anyone who claims to have enjoyed it – similar to my suspicion of those who prefer cats to dogs or who say they don't like puddings. Up to this point, the only sports day race I had been selected to compete in was the egg-and-spoon, aged five, where instead of an egg I was made to run with a King Edward potato.

Fast-forward ten years and I find myself standing in a line with four terrifyingly muscular girls, flexing their biceps and bathing their knuckles in buckets of ice, while the rest of the school stand cheering on the sidelines.

The whistle blows.

Heart thumping, palms sweating, I place the sturdy HELL BALL in the crook of my neck and hurl it with all the strength I can muster. Only to watch it sail in a perfect diagonal line, crashing through the wooden fence of the school's 'conservation area' and landing with a splash in the eco-pond.

ANYHOO, it was due to this mild dyspraxia that I managed to work my way through no fewer than three traumatised driving instructors. To give myself credit, I really don't think they were up to much. A little lily-livered, you might say.

My first instructor, Shaun, came from a local agency called Drive Hard. It soon became clear that after thirty wearisome years of teaching, Shaun's interests no longer lay in driving, but in winning the lottery and building his garden wall. Our three lessons involved me driving to Tesco for his Lucky Dip, and emergency-stopping the car every time he caught sight of any particularly large and shapely bricks.

Then my mother found Colin.

With a 100 per cent pass record and glowing recommendations from all his past pupils, Colin was a sure-fire winner.

We only made it through one lesson.

'Now, Gabrielle, you need to keep to the right on this roundabout,' he instructed, as I flicked on my indicators. 'Righto!' I beamed, pulling out to the right and proceeding to drive ANTI-CLOCKWISE round the roundabout.

It was only due to Colin's lightning-fast reflexes and the dual controls that we avoided colliding head-first with an oncoming car.

The less said about my third driving instructor the better. I believe he is now out of therapy and living in west Wales somewhere as a pig farmer.

It fell upon my poor father to take his place in the passenger seat. I would say our first outing was the worst. After my father had very generously bought me a clapped-out second-hand Ford Ka from a local garage, I ignored his offer to drive it home for me, insisting that I could do it myself. We hadn't got as far as 100 metres down the road before disaster struck.

Despite the fact that I was only doing about 20 mph, one of my magnetic L-plates suddenly blew off the front of the car, smacking with great force into the windscreen.

'I'VE HIT A BIRD!!!' I screamed, losing control of the steering wheel and swerving chaotically across the road.

Now, my father is a very calm man. The only time I ever recall him losing his cool was when attempting to erect some new curtain poles in the dining room eight years ago, which culminated in him yelling 'BUGGER, BUGGER BUGGER!' before retiring to the garden shed with a large brandy.

Yet, understandably, my driving managed to send him over the edge.

'Just stop the car, STOP THE CAR!!' he cried hysterically, slamming his foot down on some imaginary brake.

Calamity struck again about ten minutes later, when we stopped for petrol. Intimidated by the queue of cars behind me, I pulled in far too close to the petrol pump, rendering my father incapable of getting out his side. I was too hysterical to reverse and try again, so my poor father was then forced to slide out of my side after me, only to become firmly wedged between my very-far-forward seat and the steering wheel.

To add insult to injury, the two sniggering teenagers serving behind the till of the shop then had to come and work out how to move the driver's seat back.

What should have been a pleasant twenty-minute journey (we only covered three miles) actually took us two and a half hours. It concluded with me forgetting to put the handbrake on for a very steep hill, resulting in us slowly but surely rolling back into a stream of advancing traffic. My father's nerves have never quite recovered from the whole ordeal. He is still plagued by regular nightmares in which I gaily drive us into the path of an oncoming steam train.

I finally passed my test after three attempts. (Not, mind you, as bad as my mate Grace, who completed her test with flying colours only to be told by the examiner that unfortunately she had failed the eyesight test before she even got in the car.) Since then, I have so far managed to reverse into a ditch and be craned out by the RAC, knocked off seven wing mirrors and been pulled over twice for driving in a bus lane.

However, all that aside, the drive from London to Wales is one that pleases me. An open stretch of motorway on which to blast out my music and perform a three-hour concert to myself (quite often tackling all ten interlinking solo parts in 'One Day More' from *Les Misérables*), and five service stations in which to have a fag and grab a sandwich (potentially also acquiring a neck pillow, a collapsible deck chair and a car bumper sticker saying *What if the hokey cokey IS what it's all about?*).

Having managed to haggle three days off work, I pull up at my family home. It's bloody good to be back. We live in a circle of four nearly identical detached houses. The close holds many happy memories for me. Rescuing a baby hedgehog and taking her to St Tiggywinkles wildlife centre. Attempting to walk on my new stilts, falling over and chipping my front tooth on the stone wall. Skateboarding with my brother, which involved me sitting on the skateboard and him pulling me along with a wooden broom.

I open the front door, letting the familiar smells wash over me. A common sight meets my eyes: my mother vacuuming the dog.

'Stand still, Archie!' she cries, as our hopelessly overexcited Labrador spins in tight circles, trying to catch the nozzle in his mouth.

'HELLO, SWEETHEART!' she hollers over the whirring of the hoover. 'Stay still, Archie . . . Still! He's moulting everywhere. How was your drive?'

'Not too bad! Made it in four and a half hours.'

'Oh, that is good. Dad was only saying to me an hour ago THE MORE YOU WRIGGLE THE LONGER THIS WILL TAKE, OKAY?'

I smile and take off my jacket. I love my mum, although she can at times be so cringingly sensible and mumsy that I want the ground to swallow me up.

One Christmas, for instance, I persuaded her to use the self-service till at M&S and, God forbid, deliberately not pay for our plastic bags. We had got about twenty minutes along the road towards home when she pulled over with a look of panic on her face, turned the car round and started back the way we had come.

'What are you doing?!' I asked her, aghast.

'I'm going to turn myself in to customer services,' she replied fretfully. 'I can't live with this on my conscience. "Scheming Middle-Class OAP Steals Plastic Bags" is exactly the sort of thing they would enjoy splashing across the front page of the *Gazette*!'

However, sometimes she can be so mind-bogglingly care-free and entertaining that I am left in no doubt that she is my mother. Like the time I finally plucked up the courage to admit to her that I was getting a tattoo, to which she breezily replied that she might join me on her sixtieth birthday and get a Labrador tattooed on each arse cheek. Or the time I caught her bumping down the stairs on her bottom clutching an armful of laundry.

We also possess a similar flair for putting our foot in it.

The most memorable example of this occurred ten years ago, when I was a chorister in Llandaff Cathedral Choir. The choir was dominated by a short and extremely rotund girl named Elizabeth, who landed all the solo parts and was treated as royalty by the choir master. One day, after evensong, my mother happened to strike up conversation with Elizabeth's mother and congratulated her on her daughter's beautiful voice.

'Well, yes,' Elizabeth's mother remarked, bristling with pride. 'We've noticed that Elizabeth is getting rounder.'

By this, quite clearly, she meant vocally. That as Elizabeth had grown in age and experience, her voice had gained a fullness and richness of tone. Unfortunately, my mother took it to mean PHYSICALLY ROUNDER.

'Oh, I wouldn't worry,' she smiled, laying a reassuring hand on the woman's shoulder. 'I'm sure it's just puppy fat.'

I rather swiftly left the choir after that.

'Sorry, darling,' my mother continues, the hoover still blaring away. 'As I was saying, Dad reckoned that if you set off at twelve, you might well miss the WELL SIT DOWN ON THE MAT THEN motorway rush hour.'

She finally turns the appliance off.

'Now, I've made you a sandwich, but I AAAGH!'

'What?' I respond in alarm, following her gaze.

'Your arms! What happened?' she cries.

I look down at the assortment of grotesque black and blue bruises splodged haphazardly across my flesh.

'Ah, yes. Not entirely sure. Probably drunkenly walked into a bin or something. Nothing to worry about!' I smile breezily.

I can always tell when my mother is cross or worried, as her lips disappear into a thin straight line. They lose all their volume and are ingested by her face. She says it stems from her days as a primary school teacher, when this expression would have the capacity to immediately silence any children misbehaving in assembly. She marches me into the downstairs toilet.

'Steady on!' I say, as she lifts up my top, wondering whether nineteen years of living in the countryside has completely abolished my mother's sense of personal space and discretion.

'Your stomach!' she exclaims, aghast. 'It's covered in bruises too!'

I look in the mirror.

Jesus.

Used to avoiding the sight of my lard-ridden stomach at all costs, I have failed to notice the unsightly bruising around my ribs and (least-favourite-word alert) belly button. Closer inspection reveals similar bruises covering my legs and back, too. Quite frankly, standing naked in front of the mirror, I rather resemble an upright pantomime cow.

'I don't trust that surgery you're signed up to in London,' Mum says when I join her in the kitchen. 'I'm booking you in to see Dr Parsons. Lovely man. Dad went to see him about his senile warts.'

I grimace. I hate going to the doctor's and avoid it at all costs. It has a strange emotional effect on me – no matter what the problem is, whenever I'm sitting in that surgery I find myself swinging precariously between sobbing and mad hysterical laughter.

I'm lucky in the fact that I very rarely fall ill. Any viruses that find their way into my body are swiftly beaten down by a thriving immune system, boosted no doubt by years of sheep-shearing and romping around amongst various forms of animal poo. Unfortunately, though, any illnesses and ailments that I do fall prey to always seem to be slightly 'outside of the box'. One instance that sticks vividly in my mind occurred on holiday with Robyn. Having just completed our second year at drama school (and therefore penniless and traumatised), we were desperate for a few days away from London. As luck would have it, Robyn's grandparents owned a villa in Malaga, which they kindly agreed to let us stay in, rent-free, for five days in August.

We had planned for a relaxing and uneventful trip. A spot of sunbathing, a few dips in the pool and a glass or two of rosé as the sun went down. However, a mere five hours after landing, we found ourselves in a bar called Tramps, where we proceeded to get absolutely off our tits.

After numerous Screaming Orgasms (a lethal combination of vodka, Bailey's and Tia Maria), I awoke the next morning with the usual combination of raging thirst, bursting bladder and deep self-disgust. But this time there was also a new, sinister element. A searing, smarting, UNGODLY pain on my arse.

'Fuck!' I screamed in agony, waddling over to the bathroom mirror to examine myself. 'What happened last night? Did I fall off a bar stool?' Having been completely poleaxed herself, Robyn was none the wiser. In the end, the pain was so bad that I came to the conclusion I must have broken or at least chipped my coccyx.

'Have a vodka,' Robyn suggested as I painstakingly filled a bucket with ice and sat in it.

'No, a doctor,' I wheezed. 'I need to see a doctor.'

As Sod's Law would have it, my arse ailment happened to fall on a national Spanish holiday called 'The Assumption of Mary', meaning that all the local surgeries were shut.

After listening to me caterwaul in rage and agony for several hours ('The Assumption of Mary indeed. How about THE ASSUMPTION OF FUCKING GABRIELLE, AS SHE DIES ARSE FIRST?'), Robyn managed to locate an out-of-hours doctor. I use the term 'doctor' loosely. I am pretty sure he was a sexual pervert.

'In you come, ladies,' he smiled, ushering us into his surgery, which was located above a tortilla restaurant. The fact that the entire place amounted to just one room, with a bed, desk and tropical fish tank but no receptionist or waiting room should have sounded alarm bells. By this point, however, I was in too much agony to care. 'Right, let's have a look at you,' he said cheerily.

I took my bottoms off and lay face down on the bed.

To my horror, he then proceeded to bring out a HEAD TORCH from his drawer, which he strapped to his forehead in the manner of a coal miner. Robyn, who I had forced to come into the room with me, spent the entire time staring fixedly at the fish tank, trying not to laugh.

'Here we go!' cried the doctor, proceeding to face-plant into my arse, shining his torch into every nook and cranny.

'Ah,' he said eventually, 'I see now. You have an abscess. Right above the anus.'

I heard Robyn give a splutter.

'Right. Crikey,' I replied, hastily sitting up and pulling up my pants. 'And what is an abscess exactly?'

The doctor moved to his desk, gesturing for me and Robyn to sit opposite him. Instead of explaining the problem, however, he proceeded to root around in his drawer, bringing out a piece of paper and pen. We then watched in startled fascination as he began intently drawing a sketch. Initially this appeared to be a drawing of two large balloons, side by side.

Good Lord, is he actually mad? I thought to myself in horror. What's he doing – inviting us to his birthday party?

It soon became clear that this was not a drawing of two balloons. Far from it. It was in fact a diagram depicting my two gigantic arse cheeks, with a large dot in the centre to represent the abscess.

'Here we have the buttocks,' he explained, 'here the anus and here the abscess.'

I could feel the bubblings of hysteria rising inside me as Robyn made a mad, strangled sound.

'Here you go,' he said, handing me a prescription. 'The abscess should rupture in a couple of days and then you must come back and see me.'

Gasping with laughter, we staggered into the street and found the local pharmacy. I handed over my prescription.

'Ah, let me see,' the pharmacist said, putting on her glasses and holding the slip of paper up to the light. Like some hideous nightmare, I was once again met face to face with the sketch of my arse, the doctor clearly having drawn it on the back of the prescription. Unable to take any more, we both ran outside and cried tears of mirth before returning to collect my medication and waddling our way to the nearest bar.

And so, back in Wales, I find myself sitting in the doctor's surgery, with an appointment to see Dr Parsons. What is it about waiting rooms these days that they insist on having a flat-screen television playing disturbing health warnings?

Most alarming of all is a cartoon of a woman holding a large glass of wine. A speech bubble appears from her mouth saying: *I'm not an alcoholic! I only have a large glass of wine a night!* She is then joined by a fat, slovenly-looking cartoon man, who chips in with: *I'm not an alcoholic! I only have two pints every night!* The whole screen then proceeds to fill from bottom to top with bubbling alcohol, the two lardy alcoholics presumably drowned in their own booze.

I'm saved by the receptionist tapping me on the shoulder and handing me a visitor's form to fill in.

Frankly, I find some of the questions a little impertinent.

Do you smoke?

Yes, I tick, praying to God that this form doesn't find its way back to my mother.

If you've ticked yes, on average how many cigarettes do you smoke a day?

This is a tricky one, as my smoking habits differ drastically from day to day. On a normal day I can get by with just a couple, yet on a night out I might find myself easily ploughing through three packets of Camels, a shisha pipe and a large cigar.

Five, I fill in.

How many alcohol units do you consume per week?

Blimey. Who the hell knows anything about alcohol units? Now if they'd asked me how many bottles of wine I drink per week, I could have answered, with confidence and clarity, a resounding fifteen, but UNITS?!

I whip out my phone and have a Google. I learn that the average woman should consume no more than fourteen units a week.

Well, that seems reasonable, I think to myself. Fourteen glasses of wine, fourteen pints of cider. I mean, it is a BIT on the stingy side, only two a day really, but I suppose it's an attainable goal to work towards.

It is then that I realise that a unit does not equate to a whole drink. Not even close. A can of lager has two units. A large glass of wine three. A pitcher of Long Island Iced Tea FOURTEEN.

Christ. If I were to keep within these extreme and inhumane guidelines I would only be allowed four glasses of wine a week! That is ludicrous deprivation. Who do they think I am, Oliver Twist?

'Gabrielle?' a male voice suddenly calls.

I turn around.

HOLY FUCKING SHIT. Expecting some fat middle-aged doctor with a receding hairline and thread-veined nose, I am shocked to be met by one of the most attractive men I have ever seen in my life. He has swept-back blond hair, a strong Roman nose and a wide smiling mouth, and is alluringly dressed in a blue checked shirt, unbuttoned just enough to show a glimpse of suntanned flesh.

'My name's Dr Griffiths. I'll be covering all Dr Parsons' patients today,' he says, gesturing for me to follow him to the consulting room.

'BRILLO PADS!' I reply, stumbling to my feet and skidding over a musical toy bus from the children's corner.

'Dr Parsons is sorry he can't be with you,' Dr Griffiths carries on, shutting the consulting room door behind him. 'Unfortunately even us doctors need a sick day every now and then.'

'HA HA HA!' I laugh uproariously, as if he has just told the most outrageous humdinger of a joke known to humankind.

Jesus, Gabrielle, I admonish myself. Pull yourself together.

Having sat down, I show him my colourful arms.

'These are severe bruises,' he frowns, bending down to get a closer look.

'Mmm, yes, doctor,' I murmur, not giving two shits for my health and instead fantasising about Dr Griffiths slathering me in I Can't Believe It's Not Butter.

'Have you been experiencing any chest pain at all?'

'No.'

'Fainting or dizzy spells?'

'No, no dizzy spells. Only when I look at you! Tee-hee! I don't suppose you would like to accompany me to—'

'Any painful flatulence?'

There is an awkward silence in which I slowly but steadily turn the colour of a smacked arse.

'P ... p ... painful flatulence?' I laugh deliriously, hastily fanning myself with the nearest pamphlet, unfortunately entitled 'Understanding Your Haemorrhoids'. 'Doctor, please!' I jabber. 'Flatulence indeed! Ha ha ha! A LADY NEVER TELLS!'

Having thoroughly examined my bruises – including, to my horror, those on my unshaved legs – he then sits back down and flicks through his giant medical book. What is it with doctors and their books? One would hope that after seven years at medical school the knowledge would be in their heads, not in some tatty volume in the desk drawer. It's a bit like a trainee pilot putting the plane into autopilot for his entire lesson, instead using the time to eat peanut butter sandwiches and play a round of 'Pet the Panty Hamster' with air hostess Cerise.

'I think I know what the problem is,' Dr Griffiths concludes, slamming the book shut.

'Yes?' I whisper, half-hoping that he is going leap up and cry, 'YOU NEED SOME PASSION FROM THE LOOOVE DOCTOR!' before sweeping me up in his arms and taking me roughly in the phlebotomy room.

'You have scurvy,' he states, bringing me crashing back down to earth.

'Sorry?'

'Scurvy.'

'Scurvy?' I repeat, my mind boggling. 'But isn't that ...? Wasn't that something pirates got in the sixteenth century?'

'It's not so common these days, but the symptoms are the same,' says Dr Griffiths breezily, tapping away at his computer. 'A poor diet and severe lack of vitamin C are usually the cause. Do you manage to include any vitamin C in your diet?'

Hmm. I like to imagine that I have a balanced diet, but in all honesty it's a balance between gin, wine and jam roly-poly. I am not and never have been a talented cook. Sadly, my culinary skills have never really progressed from the Fisher-Price 'Laugh & Learn Learning Kitchen' that I owned at the age of four – the plastic fruit and vegetables handily halved and stuck together with Velcro.

I open and shut my mouth a few times, desperately trying to remember which foods contain vitamin C and if I have ever consumed them.

'I had an orange ... jelly the other day. And a Capri Sun,' I offer.

Dr Griffiths shakes his head.

'I'm going to be prescribing you two weeks' worth of supplements to take with meals,' he instructs. 'In the meantime, you need to make sure you eat at least five fruit and veg every day and consume absolutely no alcohol.'

There is a stunned pause as I try to digest the latter part of this sentence.

'Oh, right!' I blink in surprise. 'So just softer drinks, such as white wine, sangria—'

'I said no alcohol.'

'Oh! You mean more like beers, cider, the occasional sherry—'

'NO ALCOHOL!'

Following the doctor's orders, my parents take it upon themselves to hide all the booze in the house (I have searched high and low for the gin bottle and can only conclude that they have BURIED it), and I find myself sitting down this evening with a glass of milk.

MILK! On a Friday! I haven't drunk milk since I was about three years old. My RDA of calcium comes from piña coladas and the occasional Dairylea Triangle. I am a bit worried that my body will actually REJECT the milk and I'll start foaming at the mouth while my head does a 360. A sort of human cappuccino machine.

To add insult to injury, I am apparently not to be trusted to go out and meet the girls for dinner – the main purpose of my visit – for fear that I will start guzzling tequila.

The anxiety over missing out is almost unbearable, as I imagine Natasha relishing the opportunity of being introduced to the other bridesmaids without me.

'This is just typical of Gabs,' I can almost hear her say, flicking back her glossy brown hair and cosily passing round a bowl of steamed cabbage. 'Don't worry, Emma – us girlies are here for you.'

Having noted my misery, over the next three days my

parents take it upon themselves to throw me a fun-filled weekend VILLAGE STYLE! The rip-roaring activities include:

1. Taking the dog to the vet's to get his tick removed

The tick occurs on this morning's dog walk. I am already at the end of my tether, having watched a mind-numbingly tedious exchange between my parents.

'You've missed a bit,' says Dad, as Mum is bent over picking up one of Archie's freshly laid turds.

'Where?' she asks, standing up and looking round, bag in hand.

'There!' he says, pointing to a spot on the ground.

'I can't see anything!'

'For goodness' sake, there it is, there!' he cries, almost apoplectic with rage at this point and grabbing the bag himself. 'Oh,' he says, peering intently at the offending article, 'it's just a leaf.'

AAAAAGHHHH.

Our cocker spaniel, Freddie, loves cows. Bizarrely, the cows seem to love him back. So much so that they regularly stick their heads through the bars of the field gates and rub noses together. Unfortunately it is today's exchange with the cows that has resulted in the large and unsightly tick, right in the centre of his forehead.

Having absolutely sod-all else to do, I am not completely against accompanying my mother to the vet's. In fact, deep down, I've always harboured the fantasy that I might end up marrying a vet. I can envisage our life together – him with his hand up a cow's backside, me smoking a fag and cheering him on from the sidelines. Him arriving wearily home at 8 p.m., me waiting in the bedroom, stark bollock naked under his spare lab coat.

Anyway, as luck would have it, Freddie is seen to by a no-nonsense female vet, who does not take kindly to me nearly fainting at the sight of her needle and having to retire to the waiting room.

2. Attending the village WI craft and produce show
Oh, this is a belter!

Please find below the programme for the fiercely contested vegetable competition. Thrilling categories include: A SINGLE ONION and THREE COURGETTES. This is hotly followed by category six, for the hardcore, all-rounder, fuck-the-system kind of woman: A SELECTION OF FIVE VEGETABLES.

After sitting through a nail-biting half-hour of judging, we move on to the much-anticipated swede-rolling competition. A truly terrifying-sounding event, involving twenty farmers hurling four-stone swedes down a hill and furiously chasing after them.

As it happens, the swede-rolling competition turns out to be highly amusing. Several of the swedes take an unexpected change of direction, cannoning into nearby hedges or through the door of the local pub, and one farmer completely loses his footing, flying through the air and landing by the gates of the church graveyard at the bottom of the hill.

3. A 7 a.m. car boot sale

This is a terrifying experience.

I had cleaned out my room and agreed to part with several items of clothing and a few members of my beloved cuddly toy collection. Even as an adult, I still have a weird fetish for cuddly toys. I will often walk past a selection of stuffed animals and develop this sort of nervous hysteria, involving sweating palms and heart palpitations, until before I know it I'm standing at the counter buying three teddy bears and a life-size toy sheep.

'You'll need to have your wits about you, Gabrielle,' my mother warns me. 'These car boot sales are a cut-throat business.'

'Yes, of course,' I reply, secretly thinking, OH PLEASE. It will surely just be a few sad old ladies looking for another figurine to add to their 'Tetley Tea collectables'.

Oh how wrong I am.

Arriving at the ungodly hour of 7.30 a.m., we are tersely informed at the gates that we are 'bloody late' and told that we will have to squeeze in at the end of the west field. I can't believe the sight before me – over two hundred cars, all with their boots open. These people must have got up and parked in the dead of night!

In front of the cars is a sea of wooden tables, filled with all manner of disturbing bric-a-brac, including kitchen knives, Barbie doll heads and second-hand lingerie. I have a mild panic attack when we drive past a stall selling what look like long black whips ('These people are sadistic maniacs!') until my mother reassures me that they are merely fishing rods.

A crowd starts circling the car before we have even parked.

'Go away!' I scream, as I turn around and come face to face with an elderly lady peering in through the passenger window.

A frenzied half-hour then ensues, in which I am confronted with the task of erecting our rickety wooden table and laying out our goods while my mother barters with the customers. In fairness, I don't think bartering is my mother's forte. The transactions go a bit like this:

SCARY OLD CRONE: How much for this jacket?

MUM: Ten pounds.

SCARY OLD CRONE: I'll give you one.

MUM: Well, that's a very kind offer, but it was about sixty pounds new and it's hardly been worn, so—

SCARY OLD CRONE: Two.

MUM: Gosh, again that is very generous of you, but unfortunately I would have to ask for a little more as—

SCARY OLD CRONE: Two-fifty, final offer. And I'll leave the hanger.

MUM: Well, that does sound a little more . . .

[customer slams down £2.50 change, consisting entirely of 1p pieces, and walks off with the jacket. And the hanger]

At one point a man even bloody runs off with our screw-driver, claiming casually, 'Oh, sorry, love, I thought it was going free!'

However, the most traumatic moment comes when I eventually part ways with my beloved cuddly toy flamingo, Larry. I finally agree to sell him to a friendly-looking woman who I imagine will treasure him and treat him with the affection he deserves.

'Take good care of him,' I say through my tears as I hand him over. 'He brought me many years of joy and happiness.'

'Thanks, love,' she replies, grabbing him. 'IT'S FOR THE DOG TO CHEW.'

Eventually my three days of village arrest are over and I am allowed to make my way back to London, under strict instructions to carry on taking my vitamin supplements and stay off the gin at all costs (HA HA).

I don't know what it is about my mother, but whenever I return to London, she acts as if I am about to drive into a zombie apocalypse.

'RIGHT, I'VE PACKED AS MANY NON-PERISHABLE ITEMS AS I CAN INTO THIS BAG,' she instructs, feverishly stuffing cans of Baxter's minestrone soup and cartons of UHT milk into a gigantic IKEA shopping carrier. 'You should have enough to see you through the next fourteen days at least.'

'Thanks, Mum,' I reply, attempting to pick it up and nearly dislocating my shoulder in the process. 'What are you doing?!' I ask, as she returns from the kitchen with her hands full of ice cube bags.

'These are to keep the stuff in the cool box cold until you reach London,' she replies, dragging out the gargantuan container from its hiding place behind the dresser.

I glance inside it.

'Christ, Mum, no, I really don't need three whole cauliflowers,' I protest.

It is then that my mobile rings. I look at the screen – my agent, Steve. No. Nooo. This is it, I think. This is the moment when I'm dropped from the books and must therefore resign myself to a life of bitter resentment and amateur dramatics.

Fearing the worst, I take the call outside.

'Hey, Steve,' I answer nervously.

'Gabby!' he replies, sounding surprisingly chipper. 'How are things going?'

'Oh excellent, thanks. Working behind a bar, recovering from a recent bout of scurvy, questioning my own existence. You know, LIVING THE DREAM.'

'Great, great,' he enthuses, clearly not having taken in a word I said. 'Now, this might come as a bit of a shock,' he warns.

Here it comes, I think, mentally preparing myself for a hammer blow to the chest.

'I've just had a call from the casting director from *Hollyoaks*. Remember that part you auditioned for a couple of months back? Nurse Number One?'

Grimly I recall the rather unflattering casting call for a 'plump, plain nurse'. Yes, I remember. What the hell do they want now? To call me back in and ask me to audition for the part of a colostomy bag?

'Well, the part is yours. They absolutely loved you.'

I momentarily stop breathing.

'Pardon?' I croak.

'You've got the role, Gabby!'

I become vaguely aware of a strangled high-pitched noise emanating from my body. A bit like when you slowly deflate a balloon.

'Hello? Gabby? Are you there?'

I suddenly come crashing back to earth.

'Are you serious?' I whisper, hardly daring to believe it. 'They actually want me on the show?'

'Yes.' Steve laughs. 'I'm serious. It'll just be one day's filming, in around two weeks' time. You'll need to go to Liverpool, but we'll sort out all your travel and accommodation nearer the time.'

I explode.

'OMIGOD OMIGOD I CAN'T BELIEVE IT!' I scream. 'THANK YOU SO MUCH! You are the best agent in the world!'

Delirious, I hang up. Oh my God. My first professional acting job. In a soap. In the back of my mind appears the vague memory of the part involving just one line – 'The test was negative, John Paul . . . you don't have HIV' – but I'm too light-headed at this point to care.

In a bubble of euphoria, I sail back into the house to tell my parents the news.

They are delighted, if a little bamboozled.

'Fantastic!' cries my dad, drawing me in for a hug. '*Hollyoaks*! That's a nature programme, isn't it?'

I haven't got the heart to correct him, so I say my goodbyes, pile my stuff into my car and drive off towards London.

This is it, I think to myself, smiling dazedly and narrowly avoiding running over a rogue sheep. Years of rejection and slog have been leading up to this moment. I've finally got my big break!

Little do I realise what lies before me.

Nurse With No Name

In the precarious world of acting, it is never advisable to give up one's day job.

Unfortunately, the very day I return to London, I decide to do just that. That one phone call from Steve completely derailed me into la-la land. No longer do I see a depressingly dreary future manically chopping limes while standing in a puddle of stale lager. No longer will I find myself tearfully reciting a monologue in front of the bathroom mirror, empty gin bottle in hand, before turning to Facebook to psychopathically stalk all my drama school classmates. Hell no. Now my head is filled with dizzying images of myself accepting the prize for Best Newcomer at the British Soap Awards, releasing a fitness DVD, or at the very least selling a 'shag and tell' story to the *Daily Mail*.

Triumphantly I stroll into The Scoff, tweed waistcoat and trousers held high, in the manner of a Viking warrior brandishing his opponent's severed head, and knock on the door of Waldo's office. The term 'office' here is about as hilarious as the term 'staff toilet' – it's a horrible dingy room at the back of the restaurant full of soiled aprons, chipped coffee cups and dirty plates. Here Waldo sits, eyes glued to the CCTV surveillance on an ancient computer, checking that none of the staff are overfilling pints or avoiding putting their tips in the tip jar.

'Enter,' says Waldo, doing his best impersonation of Dr Evil.

'Hello, Waldo,' I say, pausing dramatically. 'I'm afraid I have some rather sad news.'

'IS THE LADIES' TOILET BLOCKED AGAIN?' he asks me, whipping round in his chair.

'What? No. No. I'm not on shift today.'

'Oh,' he says, uninterested again, turning back to face his screen.

'No, the thing is ... Well, sadly, it is time for me to give my week's notice. It's all happened rather quickly, really, but I've been cast in my first acting role . . . ON TELEVISION.'

I'm not quite sure what reaction I was expecting – for Waldo to gasp in shock and delight perhaps, or beg me to stay, or even shyly ask for my autograph. I was certainly not expecting him to zoom in on the image on his screen of one of the waitresses, who was no doubt handing out too large a pot of mayonnaise, before muttering unconcernedly, 'Ah, right. Well, make sure to hand in your uniform before you go.'

Hmph.

The following day I receive an exciting phone call from Steve informing me that I'll be getting the train up to Liverpool on 22 November. The actual filming will take place on the 23rd – as fate would have it, my twenty-fourth birthday. 22. 23. 24.

I am a highly superstitious person, when it suits me. For instance, normally I wouldn't have a panic attack about breaking a mirror or walking under a ladder, yet on the day of something important happening, like the EuroMillions triple rollover being drawn, I find myself throwing salt over my shoulder, knocking on wood and screaming blue murder at the sight of a black cat. So the fluke of the *Hollyoaks* filming landing on a day of such significance has me in all kinds of a flutter.

'Can you believe it?!' I shriek down the phone to my mother. 'Twenty-two, twenty-three, twenty-four! That can't be a coincidence, can it? I honestly feel like this job is a divine gift sent from Baby Jesus himself!'

Instead of my mother matching my levels of pure unadulterated joy, there is a pregnant pause at the other end of the line. This is followed by the sound of scuffling and chairs scraping, before she quite audibly hisses, 'Stuart . . . STUART! She's filming sodding *Hollyoaks* on the twenty-third! Yes! Her birthday!'

'What's going on over there?' I demand, like some riled-up librarian. 'What are you two whispering about? I can hear you, you know.'

Eventually my mother comes back on the line.

'Well the thing is, darling . . . Fabulous news about the filming date, absolutely fabulous . . . but the thing is, I'm not sure if you remember, but we'd agreed that it would be nice for me and Dad to come up to London for your birthday this year. We've got a table booked at that French restaurant you like. And tickets for *Miss Saigon*.'

Of course I have forgotten. I am the worst daughter in the world.

'Oh no, Mum, I'm so sorry,' I grovel, guilt washing over me. 'I only found out today. Is there any way you can cancel? Come another weekend?'

'Well, Dad says it's a bit late for us to cancel the train or the hotel room . . . or actually the *Miss Saigon* tickets, but not to worry, darling! It's not your fault at all. Dad and I will come up and have a nice time anyway.'

Aaagh. Anyway. No time to dawdle. There are things to be done.

Due to the highly confidential nature of the *Hollyoaks*

plotline, I am informed that my script will be delivered to my flat, BY COURIER, in a couple of days' time. I find this wildly exciting, imagining myself signing for the package under cover of darkness, then doing some sort of secret handshake in the manner of the Freemasons.

As it happens, the script ends up being shoved through my letter box at 11 a.m. the next day, along with a gas bill and a DFS sofa sale flyer, my undercover courier clearly coming in the form of the regular postman.

The days leading up to the 22nd go painstakingly slowly, as I read and reread the script, practising my one line with a variety of emotions and accents. Dad sends a jolly little email wishing me luck and letting me know that he's managed to move my *Miss Saigon* ticket to the 21st, so I can go and see it the evening before I travel up to Liverpool.

I quite often go to the theatre on my own. One of the few perks of being a single person in London is that you can grab a cut-price seat on the day of the performance, awkwardly sandwiched in the middle of a row of families and couples. The problem is, although I will save money on the ticket itself, I always end up blowing three times as much in the theatre bar, meaning that the whole evening becomes one massive solitary piss-up.

Miss Saigon turns out to be no exception. Having purchased a large red wine before the show, decanted another into a plastic cup for the first half, pre-ordered a glass for the interval then taken another one in for Act Two, by the time the curtain call arrives I am completely trolleyed. As the cast come on to take their bows, I stand up, tears unashamedly pouring down my face, whooping, cheering and trying to clap, so drunk that several times I miss my other hand and end up slapping the breast of the elderly woman sitting next to me.

Muttering that 'no one will ever love me like the soldier loved that prozzie', I gather my coat and stagger my way on to the tube home, randomly humming odd out-of-tune bits of 'The Last Night of the World' and snivelling into a slice of pizza.

It is unfortunate that I like to keep my mobile on my lap during performances. During my sozzled standing ovation it fell unnoticed to the floor and was left behind. I therefore find myself, at 10 a.m. the next morning, tearfully rapping on the door of the Prince Edward Theatre, frantically describing the item to a member of security ('It's a white iPhone, with three large cracks, possibly more after last night, and a phone case with lobsters wearing sunglasses') before catching the train to Liverpool by the skin of my teeth, phone in hand.

Having inhaled a bacon sandwich and fallen into a hung-over stupor for the majority of the journey, I am rudely awakened by a boy across the aisle from me talking very loudly on his phone.

'YAAAAAAR,' he says in a very annoying accent, probably quite similar to my own. 'Well I went for the audition and at the end the casting director said to me, "Justin, I feel like you've been brought here by magic."'

My ears prick up, and I unashamedly tune into his conversation.

'They're casting for a cruise ship next week – six months around the Canary Islands. I don't even need to audition, they know I'd be perfect.'

HA! I think to myself. Usually overhearing the nearby conversations of successful actors sends me into a spiral of depression and feelings of worthlessness, but NOT TODAY, SONNY JIM!

Ostentatiously I withdraw my *Hollyoaks* script from my bag and open it on my lap, the front page pointing in his direction. Annoyingly, he refuses to glance over.

It is at that point that my mobile rings. Steve.

'Hey, Gabrielle!' His voice blasts through the speaker. 'I've just had a call from the *Hollyoaks* team. Your co-star is apparently not very well, so they've decided to postpone your filming to next weekend. So don't get on the train yet!'

I look out of the window as the train pulls into Lime Street station.

'I'm on the train, Steve,' I say through gritted teeth, realising that I now have the full attention of not just Justin, but the entire carriage. 'And have just arrived in Liverpool.'

'Oh ... right. Damn. Bad luck there, ha ha!' He laughs nervously. 'Well, best thing to do is pop on a train back and I'll see if they'll reimburse your ticket.'

And so the night before my birthday is spent buying a tomato and mozzarella panini in Lime Street station, Liverpool, as I wait for the next train to take me back to London.

This doesn't bode well, I think to myself as I spit out

a bit of chewed-up paper that's got stuck to the melted cheese. It almost feels like someone up there is warning me off this job.

The next day I end up seeing bloody *Miss Saigon* for the second time in forty-eight hours (now a completely torturous experience without the aid of four glasses of wine), as my parents, unable to face the thought of abandoning me on my birthday, shell out for another ticket.

When I finally arrive in Liverpool the following Friday, my initial buzz and excitement about the job has turned to a sickening dread. I cannot shake the feeling I had at the station last week that something is destined to go horribly and embarrassingly wrong.

Things, however, are perked up considerably by the fact that I am spending the night in a hotel. I love staying in hotels. Even the most budget of rooms feels like a massive treat to me. I always find myself running around in a blur of excitement, opening and closing drawers, testing the springiness of the bed and marvelling at every one of the bog-standard items.

'Ooh, look at this darling little plastic kettle! With dinky sachets of long-life milk!'

'These free toiletries are amazing. Who knew that you could get shampoo, conditioner, body wash, floor cleaner and shoe polish ALL IN ONE BOTTLE?'

'Wow! A Bible! I've never actually looked inside one before, but perhaps tonight's the night!! Bring on the New Testament!'

As it happens, the hotel that *Hollyoaks* puts me up in is rather luxurious. We are talking a full-size kettle, and shampoo, conditioner and body wash in SEPARATE BOTTLES.

Steve has already told me that I need to be at the studio at 7 a.m. for costume and make-up. 'So don't worry about getting ready. Just turn up as you are!' he breezily informs me.

Like hell I will. I set my alarm for 5 a.m. in order to do a full au naturel hair and make-up routine before arriving for my actual hair and make-up. This will involve showering, shaving legs (via an entire packet of men's disposable razors), shaving armpits (with the least hair-clogged razor), plucking eyebrows into roughly eyebrow shape, dyeing moustache, freaking out at how dazzlingly blonde/albino-like moustache has now gone and then trimming it down with nail scissors, giving myself a 'big and bouncy' blow-dry, following a YouTube tutorial, and finally embarking on a make-up-free look involving foundation, blusher, highlighter, clear mascara and eyebrow pencil.

Why is it that the earlier you have to get up, the more impossible it is to actually fall asleep?

Having planned for a full eight hours, I spend the night tossing and turning, my feet tangled up in the many layers of sheets, one bloodshot eye trained on the alarm clock like a keen lizard, panicking as the hours tick by.

No sooner have I finally fallen into blissful unconsciousness than I am dragged back out of it by the sound of my alarm ringing. Blearily I peel open one eye.

6 A.M.?!! HOW IN THE NAME OF ARSE IS IT ARSING 6 A.M.?!!!

Oh my God. OH GOD.

I hurl myself out of bed and survey myself in the mirror.

Rather than appearing refreshed and well rested, I look like I've spent the night in a wheelie bin. We are talking shiny skin, insane hair and blurry eyes. Worse still, having eventually fallen asleep face down on the pillow, my fringe has formed a resolute parting in the middle, giving me the look of a 1950s public schoolboy.

Stifling a small scream, I fling open my laptop and get the YouTube tutorial up.

'Hey, guys! Thanks for all your messages and comments,' smiles some perfect-looking brunette, whom I want to punch through the screen. 'As promised, here's my next video, where I show you how to achieve the classic big and bouncy blow-dry.'

'Yes, come on, come on!' I mutter anxiously.

Smiling serenely, she then demonstrates what looks like a simple technique – pulling the brush down a section of hair, then sort of rolling it back to the top.

I pull my barrel brush down as shown, but when I roll it back up, the hair stays attached to it, locking the brush on to my scalp in a giant knot. Via a series of shrieks, I eventually manage to tug it free, forming a massive puff of cloud-like hair on top of my head.

Realising that I only have half an hour to go, I bung the whole lot into a ponytail and call a taxi.

Despite the earlier drama, it is very bloody exciting rocking up at the studios. The taxi driver knows the way with a distinct weariness, as if he is forever driving overexcited bit-part

actors there at this hour of the morning, and immediately
gets us buzzed through the main gates. There in front of
us is the Hollyoaks High School, just how it appears on TV,
and next to it, even better, a building with *Limehouse Pictures*
emblazoned across the front.

Having convinced the man behind the desk that I am
actually playing a named part and am not just an extra
(rather difficult when your character is called Nurse Number
One), I am ushered along a series of endless corridors to the
make-up room.

'Whoops, sorry,' I say, opening the door and crashing into
someone coming in the opposite direction.

'No problem,' replies a familiar voice.

I look up. Oh my God. Standing in front of me is the actor
James Sutton, who plays blond hunk John Paul McQueen.
I've had a fangirl crush on this actor since the age of eleven,
when I used to sneakily watch *Hollyoaks* while Mum cooked
dinner, flicking it over to something more wholesome, like
Blue Peter, whenever she came in the room. And in a glorious
turn of events, it just so happens that he will be acting in the
scene with me today.

I haven't had much contact with celebrities. Unless you
count my stalking of Colin Firth, or the author Terry Deary
once signing my *Awesome Egyptians* book. So although I am
well aware of who James Sutton is, I forget that he has never
seen me before in his life.

'Hello, you!' I gabble excitedly, drawing him into an
embrace. 'Long bloody time no see!'

If he is slightly frightened by this delirious, Hagrid-like girl cradling him to her breast, he is a perfect gentleman and does not show it.

'You must be my nurse,' he smiles at me, extracting himself from my arms. 'Looking forward to working with you today.'

The thought of nursing James Sutton all becomes too much for me at this point, and I stand red-faced and open-mouthed before being hurried by a make-up girl into a chair.

'Right . . .' she says, surveying the state of my hair before bringing out a paddle brush the size of . . . well, a paddle, and hacking through it with such force that I'm nearly dragged off my chair.

Make-up done, I'm then collected by a young, slightly harassed-looking assistant called Andy.

'We're in a bit of a rush this morning,' he informs me, as we weave through another warren of corridors and double doors. 'So I'll just show you to the dressing room, then we'll be going straight on to the set.'

'No problem!' I reply, panting to keep up.

There is a little niggle in the back of my mind, which I keep on hastily pushing away. A couple of weeks ago, I was called by the costume department and asked for my dress size.

'Oh, I'm fairly petite,' I told them airily. 'A slip of a thing, really! Somewhere between a size six and a size eight.'

I can only put such a flagrant fib down to my worry that upon learning my real dress size, they would cry, 'Christ, we can't hire this heifer!' and offer the role to someone else. Also, I reasoned that as a nurse I was likely to be wearing scrubs, which always look nice and stretchy on TV, so the size wouldn't matter.

'Here we go,' says Andy, ushering me through the door. 'Your costume's just on the bench there. I'll wait outside and see you in five.'

I stare at the garments in horror.

Laid out in front of me are the teeniest, tiniest pair of trousers and shirt I have ever seen in my life. Something you might find in the 'novelty' section of Pets At Home to adorn your pet gerbil with. Trying not to hyperventilate, I plaster on a jubilant smile.

'Thank you so much!' I say, going to shut the door. 'These look perfect. I'll just slip them on and see you in a sec.'

As soon as the door is closed, I silently scream at my reflection in the mirror.

Fuck. Fuck. FUCK!!! What the hell am I going to do?

Okay, deep breaths, Gabrielle. You're only a couple of sizes out. I'm sure these are good-quality clothes with plenty of stretch and give.

I quickly undress (my own garments looking like giant clown clothing in comparison) and reach for the trousers, trying not to notice the Primark label within.

What ensues next I can only liken to trying to stuff a large blancmange into a thimble.

Somehow I manage to get the clothes on, but any sudden movements and I will literally EXPLODE out of them. The only way I can actually move in the trousers is to maintain a sort of squatting position, like I'm about to lay a terrific dump.

'How does everything fit?' calls Andy through the door, clearly having taken in my size and nursing serious reservations himself.

'LIKE A BLOODY GLOVE!' I reply through gritted teeth, panting and sweating as I try to do up my fly.

I am, by this point, already starting to lose the sensation in both of my arms. The short cotton sleeves are so tight that they have cut off all circulation, horribly reminiscent of butcher's string wrapped around a piece of pork.

Finally I get the trousers done up.

'Ready!' I cry, walking bow-legged out of the door, numb arms swinging wildly.

There is a distinct pause while Andy, open-mouthed with shock, takes in the sight. But, clearly familiar with the highly sensitive nature of actors in regard to their appearance, he manages to smile feebly and say, 'Fantastic,' before grabbing a large safety pin from a nearby drawer.

'Um, I'm just going to pop this on your shirt, just to, you know, give the buttons a little extra support,' he explains, trying not to stare as my mahoosive double-D breasts heave against the confines of the cheap material. In fact, the shirt is so tight that my breasts have begun to escape upwards, forming something of a human shelf beneath my chin.

Together we walk/waddle to the set.

I consider myself to be a fairly strong-stomached girl. One has to be, growing up in rural Wales, surrounded by various forms of animal dung. But if there's one thing I cannot abide, it's blood and needles. I would go so far as to call it an actual, genuine phobia. I am the girl who needed a crash mat put down during school injections and fainted while dissecting a sheep's heart. (It didn't help that my mum had accidentally bought me a cow's heart from the butcher's, meaning that mine was twice the size of anybody else's.)

In fact, fainting has been a common problem for me over the years. I have pretty much passed out at every single blood test I've ever had. I realised that things were bad when I fainted while watching someone have a sample of their blood taken ON TELEVISION.

The worst experience was a few years ago. I had recently started having sex with my then boyfriend and, paranoid that I would soon be riddled with STIs, I quietly went to have a full sexual health screening at my local clinic. Having pre-warned the nurse of my squeamishness, I was amazed after the blood test to not only still be conscious, but to feel absolutely fine.

'Do you know,' I said, smiling as I jumped up off the bed, 'this is the first blood test I've ever had where I haven't fainted. Perhaps I'm cured!'

I then walked out of the consulting room in a diagonal line, fainting straight into a metal radiator. To my complete mortification, I woke up being hauled by two doctors and a nurse (why it was necessary for THREE of them to lift me, I'd rather not dwell on) on to a trolley, before my mother was called to come and collect me.

I knew that I would be playing a nurse on *Hollyoaks*. I knew that the scene would involve me pretending to take a sample of blood from John Paul. But I didn't think I'd actually be doing it. I thought we'd say our lines, then the screen would cut to a generic blood-taking clip borrowed from *Casualty* or *Doc Martin*.

Instead, to my horror, I am greeted on set by a real live nurse, who cheerfully informs me that she'll be teaching me how to realistically perform a rapid HIV test.

Laid out on the table in front of her are the instruments of torture – antiseptic wipes, cotton wool balls, plasters, testing sticks and (I feel a lump of bile rise in my throat) a selection of different-sized FINGER PRICKERS.

'Now don't worry,' she says reassuringly, noticing my deathlike pallor. 'We'll be using a blunt needle for the actual take.'

She waves what looks like an extremely sharp and realistic finger pricker under my nose and I feel myself break out into a cold sweat.

Keep it together, Gabrielle, I tell myself sternly, gripping the side of the table for support. This is your first ever professional role. Now really is not the time to faint, throw up or shit yourself.

Unfortunately, having lost all sensation in my limbs due to my child-sized clothing, I am already very nearly at the point of face-planting into the floor.

Around me the film crew are setting up, heaving in monstrously large lights with flaps and setting up some form of train track along the floor for the camera to slide along.

'So, Gabrielle,' says the nurse, drawing my attention back to the table of horror. 'You're going to be performing a simple

finger-prick blood test. You'll need to wipe the finger first
with an antibacterial wipe, then prick it, like this . . . '

To my dismay, she pricks her own finger, squeezing it to
allow a blob of blood to rise to the surface.

'Okay?' she asks, as I am cannoned into the corner by a
crew member carrying in a large polyester board.

'Yep, yep, fine,' I say, feeling beads of sweat erupting from
the pores on my forehead.

'Then you take the blood sample and drop it on to the
tester stick like this.' Like something out of *The Blair Witch
Project*, she smears her bloodied finger on to the stick, leaving
a large red stain, before popping her finger into her mouth
and sucking off the excess blood.

I am nearly sick all over the carpet.

'RIGHT, team!' calls the director. 'We're nearly ready for
our first take. Let's get James in.'

My co-star is hustled in, a group of flustered make-up and
costume girls fussing around him, dabbing on powder and
straightening his clothing.

He catches my eye and winks.

'Smash it,' he says.

'SMASH ME!!' I nearly cry, luckily managing to restrain
myself and muttering something incomprehensible instead
in reply.

I will never know how we made it through that scene.
Sweating and shaking, I descend on my co-star with the
needle, looking less like a gentle and calming nurse and more
like the angel of death. James tries not to look too horrified.

After about ten takes, when I finally manage to get it right, the director calls cut and everyone cheerfully spills to the canteen for lunch.

I am very well accustomed to feeling like the out-of-place 'new girl'. At the age of ten, I won a scholarship to a private school in Cardiff. Having spent six blissful years at my sweet village primary school, where educational activities amounted to finger-painting and making Easter bonnets, I was suddenly thrown into an alien world of Latin classes, hockey lessons and mental arithmetic. To make matters worse, I joined halfway through a term, meaning that I well and truly stood out like a sore thumb.

On my first day, I was horrified to discover that all the doors to the buildings had different codes on, and worse still, several were in ROMAN NUMERALS. Having got left behind after an excruciating geography class in which we had a heavy discussion about cumulus clouds (having not been taught geography at my village primary school, I'd completely missed out on the basics of the subject and still to this day cannot read a map or confidently point out where I live on the globe), I found myself panting along the corridors, crying with fear and frustration as I tried to read the different combinations scribbled in biro on the back of my hand, smeared to the point of illegibility by my own snot and tears.

Eventually, after sticking it out for three years, I asked my parents to move me back to the local state school, where I could be with Emma and all my old friends from the village.

They agreed, much to the horror of the headmaster at the
private school.

'A ... a STATE school?' he apparently gasped in dismay.
'But what about Gabrielle's Latin?' (Needless to say, I have
never got any use out of my three years' Latin training, and
to be perfectly honest, can only remember the word *minimus*,
which was the name of the cartoon mouse on the front of our
textbooks.)

Having finally escaped, little did I know that the grass
would be just as horrifying on the other side. Despite being
reunited with my old friends, I was once again the new
girl, and even worse, this time the complete posho coming
from the big fancy school. After having my uniform quickly
adjusted by a horrified Emma ('Oh my God, Gabs, you don't
DO YOUR TOP BUTTON UP! And your tie shouldn't be all
tight like that – you need to make it short and fat like this'), I
tried my best that first day to blend in.

Unfortunately, disaster struck in the form of home economics class. Having absolutely no cooking experience
whatsoever, home economics not having been deemed a
worthy subject at my previous school, I was terrified to learn
that I would be baking an apple cake.

Nervously I laid all the ingredients out in front of me on
the counter, keeping my eyes trained on my friend Anya to
copy exactly what she did. I'd only got as far as the first step –
chopping up the apples – when it all started to go wrong,
as my knife went straight through the fruit and sliced open
my finger.

It wasn't a bad cut at all, and initially I tried to hide it. Unfortunately, though, the blood started seeping into the apples, slowly turning them a ruddy shade of pink. That did it. I came round several seconds later lying face up on the floor of the classroom while a circle of students stared down at me.

'What happened?' I whispered in horror on the phone to Anya that night, having been escorted to the staffroom and then collected by my mother.

'Well, you fainted,' she replied. 'But you sort of fainted into the porcelain mixing bowl and knocked yourself out at the same time.'

After that, I managed to blend my way into state school life by keeping my head down, though the fact that I was only allowed to cook with wooden utensils significantly limited the range of dishes I was able to produce. While Lucy and the rest of my year group were whipping up coq au vin and confit of salmon, I was praised for having managed to reheat a bowl of ready-made custard.

As I walk into the *Hollyoaks* canteen, it becomes painfully clear that I am once again the floundering, out-of-place new girl. Everyone is sitting in cliques: the extras at one big table, the make-up girls on a small one and the camera crew at another. The main artists are nowhere to be seen – presumably they are sitting in their private dressing rooms being hand-fed grapes and giving interviews for *Heat* magazine. There is absolutely nowhere for Exploding Trouser Girl to park herself.

Shakily, feeling all eyes in the room upon me, I get myself a tray and queue up for some hot food.

'I'll have a baked potato and beans, please,' I say to the bored-looking serving lady, praying that a stodgy dish will fortify me for the afternoon ahead while not giving me wind. Farting on set would really be the final straw.

She shoves the potato on to a plate and slops some beans on top, before moving to the till.

'That will be four pounds fifty then,' she says.

I instantly go all hot and cold at the same time.

Stupid of me, really, but never having been on a professional television set before, I presumed all the food would be free of charge. That I could pretty much just amble up and wolf down what I wanted. And having left my purse in my handbag upstairs, I have absolutely no way of paying.

'Ooh, do you know what?' I exclaim, turning to the long, snaking queue forming behind me. 'I've just remembered . . . I'm on a diet! Yes! I'm not meant to be eating carbs at all!'

I beam at the astounded-looking dinner lady and slide my tray back towards her.

'Wait, so you don't want—' she begins.

'Sorry to have bothered you – save that one for someone else! Byeee!' I trill, then turn on my heel, bashing shoulders with the man standing behind me, and waft gaily out of the room.

Like someone who's just emerged from a traffic collision, I stagger to the toilets in a state of numb shock, before shutting myself in a cubicle and bursting into tears. Then, feeling about ten years old, I draw out my mobile from my pocket and call my mother.

'I'm all alone, Mummy!' I cry, taking huge shaky intakes of breath between racking sobs. 'Everyone knows each other, I have no one to sit with and I can't move properly in case I ERUPT FROM THESE CASTRATING TROUSERS!'

I hear someone walk into the next-door cubicle, so I quickly reduce my sobs to a quiet grizzle.

'What do I do?' I whisper.

As anticipated, my mother is full of her usual Marge Simpson-like advice.

'You stroll on over there,' she begins, 'and say, "Hello! My name is Gabrielle and I would like to be your friend!" Or perhaps you could hand something around, like a packet of Werther's Originals.'

'No, Mum . . .'

'Or I could ring up whoever's in charge and ask someone to come and sit with you, if you like. I used to do that for you when you were little. I remember when you were at Pony Club and were too frightened to use the Portaloo so instead chose to defecate in—'

It is at that moment that I hang up.

Having whiled away forty minutes in the toilets, playing solitaire on my phone and making origami animals out of loo roll, it's finally time to head back to set for the second half of filming.

This, thankfully, involves no blood, needles or any other form of medical procedure. I simply have to sit at a desk, gaze into the eyes of the beautiful James and deliver my one crucial line: 'The test was negative, John Paul. You don't have HIV.'

'Where were you at lunch?' asks James, sitting down opposite me as the camera crew set up. 'All the actors head to the green room to eat.'

FUCK'S SAKE.

'Oh, I had a few phone calls to make.' I smile breezily, tapping absent-mindedly at the computer in front of me, which turns out to be a prop, with a blank screen and the keys stuck down.

'Right, guys, we're running behind time, so I'd like to get this in one take,' the director shouts. 'Will you be all right, Gabrielle?' he asks, squeezing himself between the cameras to head over to my desk. 'You need to pretend to look up John Paul's files on the computer, give it a pause, then turn to him and deliver the line. Okay?'

'Yes, yes, that'll be fine,' I reassure him, trying not to be insulted at this staggeringly simple acting-by-numbers direction.

'Right, silence, please!' the first assistant director says. A hush falls. 'We're going for a take.'

'Speed!' calls the cameraman.

'Sound check,' says the sound guy.

'Clapper!' calls the clapper boy, running on and shouting, 'Scene forty-two, take one.'

'Aaaaand . . . action!' says the director.

Completely in the zone, I turn to my blank computer screen and scan it with an expression of what I hope comes across as concerned authority.

This is great, I can't help thinking. Look at me! A proper actor doing proper acting!

Slowly, slightly milking the moment, I look up and allow a smile to spread across my face.

'The test was negative, John Paul. You don't have AAAGH!' A sudden sharp pain stabs my left breast, and I come completely out of character and howl in agony.

What the hell has happened? Has a wasp somehow got into my bra?

I look down.

Oh no. Oh no, oh no, oh no.

Unable to take the strain of my heaving breasts any longer, the safety pin holding my shirt together has snapped open, sticking itself into my chest. I feel the eyes of the entire crew on me, staring aghast at my flopping right tit.

The filming is very quickly wrapped up after that, a red-faced Andy rushing in with another safety pin of industrial size, the sort you see holding together old-fashioned terry nappies. As my one line is hastily shot, everyone in the room avoids meeting my eye.

Having broadcast from the hills to anyone who would listen that I would be appearing in *Hollyoaks*, I then spend the subsequent few weeks desperately trying to keep the transmission date a secret.

I eventually end up letting it slip to my actress friends Robyn, Katie and Alice, who troop over to my flat to watch, armed with bags of popcorn, pizzas and a large bottle of gin to pour straight down my throat.

As my scene isn't until the very end of the episode, by the time we get there excitement levels are at fever pitch.

'Phwoar, he's a bit of all right, isn't he?' exclaims Robyn as James appears on the screen. 'Is he gay in real life?'

'No, straight. He's got a girlfriend. Who's a model,' I reply darkly, stuffing a slice of pepperoni feast into my mouth.

Suddenly the screen pans out on the waiting room of the clinic.

'This is it, this is my scene!' I scream, lurching across the floor to grab the gin bottle.

'Oh my God, oh my God!' cries Katie, moving so she's about an inch away from the television.

The camera follows John Paul as he walks nervously from the waiting room to the consulting room.

'THOSE ARE MY HANDS!' I cry, seeing a shot of my giant, clammy clown's hands administering the needle on screen. 'Does it look realistic?'

'It does, it does!!' squeals Alice.

The camera then zooms in on a close-up of James's exquisite face.

'The test was negative, John Paul,' comes my voice. 'You don't have HIV.'

Yet instead of moving to me, the camera stays on John Paul as he smiles with relief and joy.

Wait a minute, I think to myself with dread. Where is MY face?!

I feel the first pricklings of realisation as the credits roll.

'Gabs ... where were you?' Katie tentatively asks.

'They ... I think they cut me from the scene,' I mutter, mortified. 'The whole shirt-bursting scenario must have been so bad that they couldn't actually show me.'

Once I've got over the initial shame and trauma of being cut from my first and probably last ever television job, we then proceed to get rip-roaring drunk and find the whole thing increasingly hilarious.

'At least we got to see your hands!' cries Katie, hiccuping with laughter.

'Yes, they acted VERY well,' adds Robyn. 'Perhaps you could be a silent actor ... like Marcel Marceau.'

I wake the next morning on the sofa, surrounded by fag ends and pizza crusts and, rather alarmingly, wearing a pair of Marigolds, clearly having performed some sort of 'comedy hand dance' for the girls.

Oh GOD.

I've scored a hat trick: jobless, single and now a complete embarrassment to all who know me.

Worse still, instead of shrinking into hiding, I must this weekend drive down to Wales to meet Emma, Natasha and the other bridesmaids for drinks, having promised to make up for missing them last time.

Maid of Dishonour

I always slightly dread returning to my home town of Cowbridge. I especially dread a night out in the local 'hot spot', Brew Bar. This is because as soon as I set foot over the threshold, I will, without exception, find myself face to face with every single person from my secondary school. And no matter what sort of exciting and glamorous life I have carved out for myself since leaving school – moving to London, getting an agent and becoming spectacularly unsuccessful in the acting profession – I will find myself nervously slotting back into my usual lowly place in the school social hierarchy.

I was never one of the cool girls. The cool girls had a special place in the sixth-form common room – at the back, by the radiator and on the green squishy chairs. They would be joined there by the cool boys, who would yell, throw bread rolls around and dare each other to swallow one of the girls' contraceptive pills, making a great big hullabaloo while the rest of us tried to work. (I can't help wondering whether I didn't make it into the cool group because I never had the need for contraceptive pills and used words such as 'hullabaloo'.)

The uncool group had to sit on the right-hand side of the common room, by the entrance, where they were constantly in the draught and would periodically be bashed in the face by one of the 'rugger boys' kicking the door open.

My circle of friends has not really changed since nursery school. We were a mixed bunch of enthusiastic do-gooders who didn't really fit into either group, spurning the common room and choosing to spend our lunchtimes at drama rehearsals, on prefect duty or at cross-country practice. (I, of course, only engaged in the first activity.)

Cowbridge is not exactly what one would call an up-and-coming place to live. A small market town, it contains a plethora of farm shops (selling things like wellington boots, hay bales and terrifying agricultural weapons of war such as scythes, one of which my mother once purchased), an old town hall, a secondary school and a farmers' market.

When the trendy Brew Bar arrived, boasting tapas and an elaborate cocktail menu, people were quite beside themselves with horror.

'What's this fancy London muck doin' comin' round 'ere?' they protested loudly, brandishing their walking sticks as a flashy sign was erected on what had once been a shop called Quills. Which sold only quills. 'You can get a pint and a sandwich in the Three-Legged Mare ... what more do people want?'

WHAT NEXT FOR COWBRIDGE? a local paper wrote. *Strip clubs and saunas?*

But despite the controversy, Brew Bar has been a surprising hit. Open both day and night, it attracts a large and diverse crowd. Groups of mums congregate there for their morning lattes, elderly couples find themselves tucking into a lunch of braised octopus, charred aubergine and twelve-month-cured ewe's milk cheese, and after seven o'clock the under-thirties swarm in for cocktails, wine and general debauchery.

It's never really been my scene. With its little tables, high stools and squishy alcoves, it has a rather pretentious, try-hard air. I miss the nights when the girls and I would hit Bridgend. Situated only six miles apart, Cowbridge and Bridgend could not be more different. Whereas Cowbridge is all tweed coats, cobbled roads and Hooray Henrys, Bridgend is all miniskirts, bargain shops and ASBO youths. Containing three tiny, dingy 'clubs' with sticky floors, dodgy music and cheap drinks, it is where, aged seventeen, I spent my very first night on the tiles.

Being underage, I quickly (via Emma) learned how to make a ropey fake ID in order to sneak my way in. In a dark and jostling club doorway, with my boobs hoicked up to my eyeballs, it amazingly passed muster.

Emma unfortunately did not have the same luck. She had stuck her fake date of birth down with superglue, giving it a bizarre 3D effect, and the bouncer started chiselling away at the thing with his car key before loudly denying us entry to the club. Snatching her card back with a cry of 'Didn't wanna come in anyway!' Emma grabbed my hand and dragged me down the street to club number two, where she confidently presented her ID again.

'How old are you?' asked the bouncer, staring at her.

'I am twenty-two and not a day over!' She beamed at him.

'Well that's strange, love, because your ID says you were born in 1992,' he smirked nastily. 'Making you just seventeen.'

It was then that we realised the half-chiselled fake digit must have blown off somewhere on the journey, and decided to call it a night.

Six years on, I find myself showing my ID at the doorway of Brew Bar with the same level of trepidation and nerves. Due not to a dodgy card this time, but to the hideous dread of being reunited with Natasha and the rest of my year group. Ushered through, I clank my way up the vertical stairwell ('artfully' done up for the festive season with sprigs

of holly and what looks like entire apples spray-painted gold)
sounding like some jittery old carthorse, and catch sight of
myself in the long mirror. Aaargh. What on earth possessed
me to wear a metallic skirt? On a skinny girl they look fantastic. I, on the other hand, look like a large Aunt Bessie's
Yorkshire pudding about to go into the oven. Hastily tug-
ging it down and sucking in my stomach, I push open the
door to the bar.

Every head turns to stare at me.

Suddenly, every single embarrassing thing I ever did at
school comes flooding back, magnified and more horrific
than ever before. The time I gave a speech about battery hens
and started crying. Performing that Katie Melua song in the
school Eisteddfod and realising during the opening bars that
I had clean forgotten all the words (then making them up as I
went along, in some gibberish/elvish language). I even catch
the eye of several people I attended primary school with,
who went on to different secondary schools. William Davies,
for instance, who sat next to me in Year 4. One day, having
made it into school with a very bad cold, I sneezed and sent
a long stream of green snot flying through the air to land on
William's desk, causing him to scream and throw up.

Oh God. Oh God, oh God, oh God.

'Gabs!' comes a cheerful, blissful voice I would recognise
anywhere. I turn to see Emma waving from a table at the
back. Next to her is Natasha, smiling coolly, and two girls
who I guess are the other bridesmaids.

Squeezing myself through the tables with an endless cycle

of 'excuse me', 'sorry' and 'thank you so much' (even managing to get my jacket caught on the back of a chair and loudly dragging it about two feet with me), I make it to the table.

'Yaaay!' cries Emma, leaning across Natasha to give me a huge hug. 'I'm so glad you could make it!'

'Wouldn't have missed it for the world!' I beam. 'Hi, Natasha.'

'Hey, Gabs.' She stands up and gives me one of those hugs that involve minimal bodily contact, more of a lean-in, as if doing a wall push-up. 'Nice to see you.' This is almost convincing, until I see her quickly glance around the bar, checking that no one overheard her.

'These are the other two bridesmaids, Louise and Ceri.' Emma introduces the girls.

'Oh my God, I love your skirt,' enthuses Louise. 'I went to try one on in H&M but they didn't have any size eighteens in stock, only eights and tens. I said to the shop girl, "Love, where do you think we are? This is Bridgend, not fuckin' Milan. Girls round here have big tits and big arses to match, sort it out."'

Louise, I decide, is going to become a firm favourite.

'Right, who needs a drink?' I ask, looking round the table.

Louise and Ceri signal to their full glasses.

'Me and Em have to be up early, so we're not really drinking much tonight,' pipes up Natasha.

'What?' I ask, whipping around to face Emma.

'Yeah, we're off for a girlie shopping trip in Cardiff,' continues Natasha, smiling in what I imagine she thinks is an attractive and angelic way, but which actually makes me want to clout her round the head with a nearby candelabra.

'I'll come with you to the bar,' says Emma, looking distinctly uncomfortable.

'Sorry,' she whispers as we make our way over. 'I didn't even know we were going until this morning. She kind of forced it on me.'

'Oh, right!' I reply in an overly bright voice, asking the barman for a large gin and tonic.

'To be honest, I'd rather be having a piss-up tonight with you.'

'Well, why don't you?' I implore. 'Come on, Pegleg. These are our salad days! I've come all the way down from London for this. Don't let Natasha tell you what you can and can't do, the old witch.'

Whoops, that slipped out.

'Oh, all right,' she relents, suddenly grinning. 'Fuck it – a couple more drinks can't hurt. I'll have a Long Island Iced Tea, please.'

The barman nods, before proceeding to bring out a staggering assortment of spirits from below the bar.

'All the whites it is, Gab,' says Emma, winking knowingly. 'Tequila, vodka, rum and gin. All the bloody whites.'

'Actually, make that a pitcher,' I tell the barman. 'I'll go halves with you.'

Natasha looks distinctly put out as we stagger back to the table, Emma carrying a gigantic jug while I clutch a large gin and tonic and five glasses.

'We weren't sure if anyone else fancied some, so got you all glasses anyway,' I beam, setting them out on the table.

'Ooh, me please!' says Ceri, looking distinctly more cheerful.

'Fucking bang on, tidy. Nice one, girls,' says Louise.

Only Natasha looks boot-faced.

'I'll just stick to my vodka soda, thank you,' she says icily.

I glug down my gin and tonic so quickly that it spills either side of the glass and down my chin, then cheerfully fill four glasses from the jug.

'Well, cheers!' I say. 'Here's to the wedding!'

Feeling the evil eyes of Natasha boring into me, I excuse myself and head to the toilet. No sooner have I locked my cubicle door than two girls clatter their way in.

'There are so many people from school here tonight,' comes the unmistakable voice of Leanne Holmes, who a) was one of the biggest bitches in our year, and b) has a very pronounced pantomime lisp.

I've actually known Leanne since I was about six years old, due to her living nearby and attending the rival primary school, but although she was a pal of Emma and Natasha, she was never one of mine. I'll never forget the time in Year 3 when she invited Emma and Natasha over after school and then proceeded to ask them, 'Why are you friends with Gabby when she's so fat?' Which was then relayed to me with great glee by Natasha next morning as we queued up for assembly.

Thrust together at secondary school, I was relieved to see that her bitchiness had taken her away from our friendship group and elevated her to the ranks of the popular girls, something I found somewhat surprising given that she still spoke as if she had a large sock in her mouth.

'I know,' replies her friend, who I recognise as a girl called Sophie. 'All the weirdos.'

They both give a horrible tinkling laugh.

'Did you hear that Emma Randall is getting married?' asks Sophie.

I sit transfixed on my toilet seat.

'Yeah, her mum told my mum,' says Leanne. 'There's no way I'm going.'

YOU WON'T BE FUCKING INVITED, I think to myself, outraged on Emma's behalf.

'Me neither,' says Sophie.

YOU'RE NOT FUCKING INVITED EITHER, I think again, further outraged.

'I don't recognise those girls sitting with her,' continues Leanne. 'Apart from Natasha Jones.'

'And Gabby Fernie,' chips in Sophie.

'Oh yeah . . . who could forget Gabby Fernie?'

They both give that disgusting tinkling laugh again. Somehow I get the feeling that these are not going to be fond memories.

'What's she doing now, anyway?' asks Leanne.

'Not sure . . . we're not friends on Facebook,' replies Sophie. 'I heard someone talking about her, though.'

YES! I think to myself with glee. Finally my time to shine. All those years of Leanne sneering at my school plays and laughing at the poem I once performed in assembly will be worth it when she hears that I left the rest of them behind in Wales and went on to train at a top London drama school.

'Apparently she went to—'

'Do you have an eyeliner?' interrupts Leanne.

I listen in agony as Sophie laboriously roots around in her bag before finally locating one.

'Here you go.'

'Cheers. Sorry, you were saying?'

'Oh yeah – Gabby. Apparently she moved to London ...'

Yes!

'Oh, right.'

'To go to ...'

Come on ... come on!

'Drum school.'

AAARGH.

'Drum school?' says Leanne incredulously. 'I didn't know she played the drums.'

'Me neither,' says Sophie. 'Oh well, she's always been weird.'

And with that they leave the toilets.

I sit, blinking in shock and trying to digest what has just happened. Surely people do not actually believe that I went to London to embark on a career in DRUMMING?

I am then forced to sit for a further ten minutes as more and more people I recognise come in and out of the toilet, complaining loudly that someone is 'taking forever in the first cubicle' and angrily hammering on the door, rendering it impossible for me to emerge.

When I eventually escape and head back to the table, I

am pleased to see that the girls are already halfway down the pitcher of cocktail, and unsurprised that Natasha is still nursing her nearly full, and surely warm, glass of vodka soda.

'BITCHTITS!' hollers Emma, quite clearly already three sheets to the wind. 'Where have you been?'

'Just to the loo,' I reply, sloshing my glass full of cocktail, which now appears to be mostly ice and six slices of lemon. 'I'll get us another jug.'

'My turn!' hollers Louise cheerfully, grabbing Ceri's hand and dragging her to the bar.

Awkwardly, Natasha, Emma and I find ourselves alone at the table.

'I'm thinking we should go to Bridgend,' Emma declares, slapping the table with the palm of her hand.

'Yes!' I cry, thrilled at this turn of events.

Natasha looks furious.

'We can't go to town, Em, RE-MEM-BER?' she says, spitting out each syllable as one might spit out olive pits. 'You're staying at mine because we have to be up early.'

'Stay at mine!' I pipe up, thoroughly enjoying sticking an oar in. 'I'll drive you over to Natasha's in the morning.'

If looks could kill, Natasha would have lasered me dead with both eyeballs.

Having tried and failed to persuade Louise and Ceri to join us, and waved Natasha off in a hilariously black mood, Emma and I stagger into the local Tesco to get provisions for the fifteen-minute bus journey.

'I'll have a bottle of Glen's Vodka, please,' I wave airily behind the counter, 'and twenty Marlboro Lights and a box of matches.'

'Matches?' comes Emma's incredulous voice behind me. 'Jesus, Gabs, what are we, CAVEMEN? I'm sure we can splash out on a lighter!'

By the time we make it to town, Bridgend is in full swing. Linking arms, just as we did when we were seventeen, we teeter our way to the best club, pausing to tug Emma's stiletto heel out of a drain cover and sling our empty vodka bottle on top of a towering pile by the bin. I don't know whether it's being home, or being on my own with Emma, or (more likely) the litre of spirits sloshing around in my system. But for the first time in a long while I feel truly and utterly happy. I want to be standing arm in arm with my best friend, both of us completely poleaxed, for the rest of my days.

And then it comes to me, with a stab: this is possibly one of our last nights out together as free women. In a matter of months Emma will have more important things in her life to worry about, such as hanging baskets and vinyl flooring, rather than standing under the nearest lamp post and asking me if her fake tan looks orange.

I vow that tonight we are going to have the best night together ever.

Things never do quite go to plan, do they?

The problem is, Emma and I have a habit of getting separated while in town. It will be due to something completely innocent, like me going to the toilet, or to the bar for drinks, but she will completely lose her shit when she can't find me and send a barrage of increasingly irate and abusive text messages. It has become almost a staple of our 'mornings after', lying in bed next to one another and howling with laughter at the messages on our phones.

I love mornings after. I'm not talking the one-night stand kind, which involve desperately trying not to wake the person next to me while I call myself a cab and hunt under the duvet for my pants. I'm talking the ones after a night out with the girls, when you all wake up on the floor of the same bedroom in various states of undress – fake eyelashes halfway down your chin, wearing pyjama bottoms and one stiletto – then in a mixture of gleeful shrieks fill each other in on the evening's antics before lumbering downstairs for a round of tea, toast and *Takeshi's Castle*.

Tonight, for the first hour, Emma and I manage to stay together pretty well, pushing our way to the front of the bar and ordering two large vodka and lemonades. Handing over a tenner, I am frankly flabbergasted when the barman hands me back five pound coins. Good old Wales.

Now then, I know that I am not the only girl to keep money in her bra on a night out. Frankly, with breasts my size it's like having two extra handbags strapped to your chest. But I think the idea is to perhaps sexily tuck a spare twenty-pound note down your cleavage, rather than £7.62 in coins, which is what I am by this point carrying. Quite often, when undressing at the end of a night, I will take off my bra to see several imprints of the Queen's head tattooed on my breasts. Worse is when I store things by accident – and not just in my bra. Like the time I went for a daytime drink with a friend and found an entire stick of cigarette filters caught on the inside of my tights.

After about an hour of drunken dancing, which involves a lot of 'FUCK OFF, YOU MUNTER!' from Emma to the surrounding men and 'HI, MY NAME'S GABBY AND I'M SINGLE' from me, I yell in Emma's face that I am going to the loo and signal for her to wait for me.

I love club toilets. I especially love club toilets in London, where there will undoubtedly be a toilet attendant for me to befriend. Unable to pass by without purchasing something, by the end of the night I will find myself wearing a jazzy new pair of flip-flops and a candy necklace, sucking a lollipop and reeking of about five different perfumes.

In Wales, toilet attendants are not quite so common. Instead, there's always a drama unfolding amongst a group of girls, while the rest of us try to offer help and drunken advice. Tonight is no exception.

'SHE'S A FUCKING SLAG!' sobs a girl with mascara streaked down her face, as the rest of her friends pour wine into her mouth, sling drunken arms around her and touch up their make-up in the mirror. 'She had her tongue down his throat and his hand was up her fuckin' skirt. I hate them both.'

'I'm gonna go out now and fuckin' knock 'er block off,' says her friend in an alarmingly soothing and consoling voice. 'Just need to take a slash.'

I cannot have been gone for more than fifteen minutes, but when I come back, Emma is nowhere to be found. I look at my phone and, sure enough, see three missed calls and five text messages flashing:

Hey gab where r u xxx

Where you at?

GAB WHERE THE FUCK ARE YOU?!!!

CMON NOW GAB DON'T PLAY GAMES WIT ME!

Goin home. Getting a taco.

Pushing my way out of the club, hiccuping and swaying on the pavement, I call Emma back. I am expecting a barrage of abuse, but she sounds remarkably cheerful.

'Heeeyyy, Bitchtits,' she says. 'Did you get back okay?'

'I'm still here, at the club!' I slur back. 'Only went loo. Where you buyin' taco from? Love tacos!'

'Oh shit, sorry,' she says, letting out a small belch down the phone. 'I meant taxi. Too pissed, need to go to bed.'

I stagger back into the club and stand swaying on the dance floor for several minutes before deciding that I should really go home myself. Stopping off at the local Chinese for a bag of crispy beef and spring rolls, I lurch my way over to the taxi rank, wondering unconcernedly which of them is going to let me in.

''Iya, Gab!' one of the drivers suddenly calls, rolling down his window. ''Aven't seen you in a while!'

'Been up blurry London,' I hiccup, shoving a spring roll into my mouth. 'Stupid London.'

'Need a ride?'

'Yes.' I nod with my eyes shut, trying to dredge up in my memory the address of the house I have lived in for the past twenty-three years.

'Twenty-four Lime Tree Grove, isn't it?'

'Tha's one.'

Having nodded off for the ten-minute taxi ride, I stagger up the drive to my front door, rooting around for my keys.

'Nooo,' I moan, emptying out on to the doorstep the entire contents of my handbag, which consists of purse, phone, empty fag packet, tampons, sea of one-pence coins and a plastic spoon. Pulling out the bottom of my bra, I then shake out all the change. Still no keys.

Feeling rather giggly and hysterical now, I decide there is nothing for it but to wake up my parents.

Why oh why I didn't just call them from my phone, I will never know.

Instead, going round to the back garden, I pick up a handful of pebbles from the rockery and, with surprisingly good aim (amazing, frankly, given my failed shot-putting exploits at school), throw them up at my parents' window. Seeing a light go on in their bedroom, and not wishing to alarm them, I then proceed to call out, 'RAPUNZEL, RAPUNZEL! LET DOWN YOUR HAIR!'

I am hustled into the house by my mother (my father presumably too seething to come downstairs) while I haphazardly try to explain to her why the contents of my handbag are all over the doorstep. Saying that we will 'talk about it in the morning' (never have a more ominous six words been uttered), she then tucks me into bed with a glass of water, as she used to do when I was six years old, before I fall into a dark and dreamless sleep.

How to Disgrace Oneself

Oh Lord
I have sinned

I wake up the following morning looking and feeling like a stubbed-out cigarette.

What in the name of arse happened last night?

Glancing down, I am pleasantly surprised to note that

I am wearing my pyjamas. Phew. Can't have been too hammered if I managed to get myself changed. Normally I wake up stark bollock naked and spreadeagled on top of my duvet.

Feeling like a small and prickly creature has crawled in and died at the back of my mouth, I reach over to my bedside table and am both astonished and thrilled to find a large glass of water sitting there. What a turn-up for the books! Not only did I manage to get changed, but I was compos mentis enough to go to the kitchen to pour myself a glass of water. Perhaps I even made myself a light yet nourishing snack and bid my parents goodnight?

Feeling much better about the whole thing, and deciding that I must have simply left Brew Bar and got an early taxi home, I shakily swing my legs off the bed, intending to locate my phone.

It is then that I find myself standing in a bowl. A large rectangular plastic washing-up bowl placed on the floor. Several towels have been spread out to cover the carpet, a bit like the way one lays newspaper out on the floor when house-training a new puppy.

That's odd, I think. Mum used to do that for me when I was little and had a stomach bug.

At the thought of my mother, it suddenly hits me.

The Long Island Iced Tea. Pissing off Natasha. Bridgend. Losing Emma. Losing my keys. Losing my marbles. THROWING STONES AT MY PARENTS' WINDOW.

Oh God. Oh God, oh God, oh God.

I'm just going to have to brazen it out, I decide. I shall nonchalantly go downstairs, thank my mother for letting me in and somehow convince them that throwing stones was the most practical and sensible way of getting their attention in an emergency. Something I saw on *Bear Grylls: Mission Survive*, perhaps.

Head spinning and acid reflux rising, I grasp hold of the banister and very slowly lower myself down the staircase.

Already I can hear the sound of my parents murmuring in the kitchen. This can't be a good sign – it's gone 9.30 a.m. This is the time they walk the dogs or go to Tesco to buy a baguette and the paper. They must be waiting for me.

'Morning, all!!' I croak cheerfully, hastily regaining my balance as I skid on a dog chew. The silence in the room is deafening.

'Eat your Weetabix, Stuart,' Mum mutters to my father, as I pull up a chair at the table.

I shakily reach for the box of Coco Pops, trying to maintain an air of normality. Oh God, I cannot handle this. I would rather stuff this entire box of cereal up my arse than eat it.

My mother finally breaks the silence.

'We're worried about you, Gabrielle,' she says. 'What on earth happened last night?'

'Lost my keys,' I mutter.

I mean, frankly I think they're making far too big a deal of this. Given that I once lost my car keys in town and they had to tow my car the twelve miles home the next morning, this is a walk in the park.

'It's Emma's wedding next year,' my mum points out, as if I could forget. 'It seems like the entire village is going – Phil and Chris from next door, the whole of the WI, even Mrs Brighton, your old school dinner lady.'

'God, not Mrs Brighton,' I say through gritted teeth.

'Yes, that's right. The one who always told you off for having your shoelaces undone and hiding your vegetables under the dinner table. They're all so excited to see you again. It's time to start taking responsibility for your actions, not go blowing yourself around like some drunken sailor.'

I stick my head in my cereal bowl to hide my snort of laughter.

'It's not funny,' she says, reaching into her bag. She brings out three books and slides them across the table to me. 'I found these in the library. Now I know you're probably going to take one look and pooh-pooh them. But you should give them a try. They look like a great read.'

I groan inwardly. My mother and I differ slightly in our literary tastes. What have we here? I wonder. *How to Papier-Mâché Yourself a New Wardrobe? Fifty-Six Exciting Things to Do with Root Vegetables?*

I stare at the covers in horror.

The books are entitled *The Ladies' Book of Etiquette and Manual of Politeness, Her Ladyship's Guide to the Queen's English* and *The A–Z of Modern Manners.*

Oh, dear God. My parents are hoping to transform me into a LADY.

What is this, *Pygmalion?* Am I soon to have marbles shoved

in my gob and be made to recite the alphabet? Taken to the races wearing a variety of hats? Engage in late-night horseplay with some Henry Higgins-like figure, while singing 'I Could Have Shagged All Night'? (Okay, I'm not entirely 100 per cent on the plot.)

Sulkily I push aside my untouched cereal bowl and stomp back upstairs to the bathroom, where I sit in my usual hangover spot next to the toilet and glare at the books.

Deciding that *The A–Z of Modern Manners* looks by far the most appropriate volume, given recent events, I flick through and begin reading. I mean ... it is an absolute bloody hoot. Here are some of my favourite pieces of advice, and how I myself have managed to reflect them so far in my daily life:

1. BEING EMOTIONAL
Don't get sentimental or try to get your man to say something he doesn't want to by working on his emotions. Men don't like tears, especially in public places.

YES, WELL ... Once on a first date, I got rather drunk and maudlin about my recently deceased dog, Teddie. Via a series of hideous flashbacks, I remember raising my wine glass and hollering, 'A TOAST TO TEDDIE!' before attempting to sing the first few lines of 'You'll Never Walk Alone'.

I think it was at that point that my date called me a taxi.

2. DRINKING
Never get drunker than your love interest, and know your limits – a

graceful lady is always alert to the warning signs of impending intoxication and ready to go home before an enjoyable evening ends in tears.

HA DE HA HA ROFLS LOLZIES OHHHH WHERE ON EARTH DOES ONE BEGIN.

The time I sat on someone's front doorstep with a traffic cone on my head and declared, 'I'm a gnome and I'm not going home'?

Perhaps three weeks ago, when I brought a family of four Hungarians home for a nightcap and a game of charades?

The thing is, I *know* my limits. I just choose to exceed them.

The instance that sticks vividly in my mind, like a small yet persistent turd bobbing stubbornly in the toilet, is a night I spent at The Buffalo Club in Cardiff.

It was a most pleasant evening up until the arrival of my ex, who I hadn't seen since our break-up a year before. I mean, I think I kept it together pretty well. Enquired about normal things, such as what he was up to now, and 'Does your grandmother still knit those adorable little bonnets?'

But of course the moment his back was turned, I staggered up to the bar like a cow on Rohypnol and wheezed, 'Mix me your strongest cocktail and then BRING ME FIVE OF THEM.'

The next thing I remember is waking up in the girls' toilets. It was eerily quiet. Yes, that's right, you guessed it. The club had locked up and gone home for the night. Tables and chairs stacked, the lot.

I was eventually let out by a lovely cleaning lady and then found by my friends an hour later in Burger King, eating a Double Whopper.

3. INTERNET DATING

Choosing your date in much the same way as you pick dishes from a menu lacks the finesse and subtlety of traditional courtship, but it opens you up to a world of possibility unavailable through conventional channels.

Ah, internet dating. Yes.

After hearing several rave reviews and success stories from friends, I finally succumbed to the pressure and joined plentyoffish.com.

They say 'fish' . . . I say PLENTY OF FUCKING BATSHIT CRAZY WEIRDOS.

I lasted four days before deleting my account, mentally scarred by the experience.

The final straw came when I received a private email from a guy asking me to be his 'submissive' – this was at the peak of the *Fifty Shades* craze. His profile picture was a man in a business suit, with no head. (I mean that it was cropped out, not like a severed head.) Attached to the email was a seven-page document listing my 'duties', including the line 'You will be rewarded for sexual acts with whipped cream and vegetables.'

I decided not to meet him.

4. TATTOOS

The upper classes normally abhor or shun tattoos. You should do the same.

Whoops.

5. SMOKING

These days an attachment to nicotine has to be very strong indeed if you are going to withstand the social pariah status of the smoker. Do not start.

Whoops.

6. SWEARING

The foolish and wicked practice of profane cursing and swearing is a vice so mean and low that every person of sense and character despises it.

Double fucking whoops.

I snap the book shut and close my eyes briefly, leaning my head against the cool wall tiles. There is a gentle knock on the door, and Mum sticks her head round.

'Just came to see if you're okay,' she says, handing me a fresh glass of water and two paracetamol.

'Thanks, Mum,' I reply, taking them from her gratefully.

'Now we need to be leaving in half an hour, but if you're not feeling up to it, I'm sure she won't be offended.'

'What?' I ask, head snapping up. 'Who won't be offended? Where are we going?'

'Nana's Christmas party, remember?' she says, incredulous

that I have forgotten. 'You offered to come with me this year. I did warn you that you might not be feeling up to it . . .'

Fuck-fuckity-fuck.

'No, of course I am, I can't wait!' I gabble, overcompensating wildly. 'I'll just quickly hop in the shower and get dressed.'

There is only one other woman in our family who behaves as outrageously and bawdily as I do. It is, rather improbably, my grandmother, Edna.

My earliest memory of her is a family trip to the beach when I was around four years old. A strong believer in wartime frugality, Nana had chosen to knit herself a swimsuit for the occasion. Yes, that's right. KNIT HERSELF A SWIMSUIT. Out of WOOL.

Ignoring the protests of those around her, she proceeded to gaily wade into the sea, completely submerging herself before standing up to give us all a cheery wave. Unfortunately, having absorbed about two gallons of water, it was at that moment that Nana's swimsuit shot downwards, leaving her standing butt-naked in the sea, bar a mass of brown seaweed draped jauntily over her shoulders.

I don't think I, or the thirty or so other people on the beach, have ever quite got over the shock.

Yet in contrast to me, Nana (who for some reason has always insisted on this being pronounced NanAR, in a rather formal and high-handed way) never has to suffer the consequences of her actions.

She does not spend her mornings scanning WhatsApp and Facebook with one eye closed, dreading what inappropriate declarations of love her drunken alter ego may have sent. She doesn't find herself breaking into a cold sweat when '8 tagged photos' flashes up on her phone and she is greeted by the sight of the smiley face she decided to draw on her chest last night, her nipples forming the eyes. She doesn't open her emails to find not only a fifty-pound Uber fare, but also a personal review she has left of the driver, describing him as a 'wise, witty and beautiful man, with an excellent command of the steering wheel'.

No.

Nana is eighty-seven years old and therefore licensed to do whatever the fuck she pleases.

Beside our mutual penchant for completely horrifying all those around us, Nana and I also share the lack of a natural aptitude for driving. At the age of eighteen, my mother bought herself her first motorbike (a terrifying thought in itself) – a state-of-the-art Honda 90. Having taken it for a spin around the block, she decided to allow my grandmother to have a go, safely within the confines of their back garden.

What then followed plays like an Ealing comedy sketch. After completely over-revving the engine, Nana shot off across the garden like a bat out of hell. Meanwhile, my very reserved grandfather apparently watched the whole scene unfold in utter horror, calling out, 'You shouldn't be on that thing, Edna!'

Unable to brake, she continued to plough on in ever-decreasing circles, before finally crashing to a halt through the runner beans. My grandfather, whose vegetable patch was his pride and joy, retired to the house with a face like thunder.

Forty years on, things have not improved. Due to trouble with her legs, and having written off her car (she put it into reverse, got her foot stuck on the accelerator and shot out of her driveway and straight into the opposite neighbour's garage door), the nursing home bought Nana a wheelchair. But this was no ordinary wheelchair. We are talking the Nimbus 2000 of motorised mobility scooters. Complete with alloy wheels, leather seat, headlights and probably an iPod dock, the thing had more horsepower than my actual car. We are talking from nought to thirty in about five seconds.

'If you can drive a car, Edna, you can drive this,' the nursing home manager declared, showing her the brakes and (God help us) speed controls.

Well, given her history, we should have anticipated what would happen when she took the wheelchair for its first spin.

Launching off at about 20mph, Nana was unable to find the brakes and exploded like a cannon ball out of the door of the nursing home, across a busy main road and into the wall of the cricket club opposite. Uninjured, she dusted herself off and swore never to ride such a 'beastly machine' again.

Nana currently resides at Applewood Manor, a nursing home about a mile from my parents' house. One generally grimaces at the words 'nursing home', imagining puréed suppers, lonely games of bridge and an overriding scent of urine. Well, I can tell you now that Applewood Manor is a whole other kettle of fish. Given the chance, I would happily surrender my dingy flat in London to live there.

Set in three acres of grounds, it is a beautiful old honey-coloured Georgian building – something you might expect to see in the National Trust handbook. Residents enjoy silver service meals, in-house classical concerts and plasma screen TVs. And every year, Applewood Manor hosts a Christmas party, where family and friends are invited for a three-course slap-up meal.

So, despite feeling on the verge of a coma, I keep my promise and accompany my mum to the celebrations.

It is a beautiful set-up. Round oak dining tables covered in crisp white cloths are adorned with twinkling candles and huge bunches of red poinsettias. In a corner of the room, a pianist sits at a baby grand, playing an exquisite arrangement of Bing Crosby's 'White Christmas'.

'Isn't it lovely, Mum?' I smile, taking in the touching sight of the elderly residents in their Sunday best proudly introducing one another to their sons, daughters and grandchildren. 'It's all so peaceful and calm.'

'OH THERE YOU ARE!' comes my grandmother's piercing cry as she is wheeled in with great difficulty by a young nurse. Nana is clutching a glass of sherry to her chest and is, quite clearly, already on a bender.

'Cooee!' she trills, giving the pianist a coquettish wave. The pianist flashes her a friendly smile of recognition and carries on playing. 'COOEE, I SAID!' Nana barks, making the whole room jump.

'Yes, hello, Edna!' The pianist waves back hastily, knocking a sheet of music off the stand.

'That's my boyfriend, you know,' Nana informs us proudly, leaving us momentarily lost for words.

After a great deal of huffing and puffing, we manage to manoeuvre Nana into a position she is satisfied with. Martha, the lovely head carer at the home, squeezes herself between the tables to say hello.

'Lovely to see you both again.' She smiles at us with genuine warmth. 'So pleased that you could make it.'

'Gosh!' she says, turning to face Nana. 'Don't you have a lovely-looking daughter and granddaughter, Edna?'

'You need to lose some weight, my girl!' comes Nana's reply, as she slaps Martha heartily on the bottom. 'You can barely fit between the tables!'

'Mum!' my mother whispers, aghast. 'You can't say things like that, it's rude!'

Unfortunately, fortified by half a glass of white wine, Nana is on a roll.

'Oh dear, there's poor old what's-her-face,' she says in an incredibly loud stage whisper, pointing very obviously at the woman sitting on the opposite side of our table.

'You mean Caroline?' my mother says. 'Why, what's wrong with her?'

'Well, her husband died two weeks ago,' declares Nana, tucking into her melon starter. 'In fact I'm quite surprised she's made it here at all.'

'Robert hasn't died, Mum. Look! He's sitting right next to her!'

Mum points to a smiling man who is very much Caroline's husband and, more to the point, very much alive.

'No, no, the poor bugger died the other week,' persists Nana, carrying on with her food. 'Heart attack, I think.'

Although she is usually an endlessly kind and tolerant person, I can sense even my mother's patience starting to wear thin.

'But he's SITTING. RIGHT. THERE, MUM!' she whispers. 'Look! With the blue dinner jacket and the glasses! You know Robert – he's popped in to see you lots of times!'

Nana finally puts down her fork and looks at Robert properly, staring at him with what will surely become an expression of joy and recognition.

'Well, I'm afraid we'll have to agree to disagree on that one, dear,' she replies. 'Oh look, here comes Malcolm!'

Next thing we know, an elderly man has bashed his way through the tables and seated himself to the left of me.

'Gosh, you're a damned fine minx,' he says, staring at me in wonder.

Although outwardly aghast, I can't deny that it is refreshing to receive some positive male attention.

'Hello, my name's Gabrielle.' I smile.

'You remind me of my old mare, Phyllis,' he continues, slightly spoiling the compliment. 'Same legs.'

'Lovely.' I smile again, trying not to take offence.

'She one of yours, Edna?' he hollers across me to Nana. 'Thought as much.'

He turns to me again and gives a hugely flirtatious wink.

'You'd take a fair amount of bridling, I'm sure!'

Worried that things seem to have taken a slightly sexual, if equine, turn, I am thankful to be interrupted by the arrival of the main course.

'What on earth is this?' asks Nana, staring aghast at her food, as if she has just been presented with a plate of Pedigree Chum.

'It's fish, Nana,' I explain. 'Hake.'

'What?' she hollers, each sip of wine appearing to raise her voice by about two decibels.

'Hake,' I repeat patiently.

'Cake? Oh, I like cake,' she replies, picking up her dessert spoon.

'No, Nana. HAKE!!'

'What's this bit then?' she asks, prodding the white flesh of the fish. 'The icing?'

Once we have eaten our fish (Nana remarking that it needed a good deal more sugar), it is time for the Christmas quiz. Each table forms a team, and I am relieved at the chance to be able to communicate with some of the arguably more sane and agreeable guests.

'First question!' calls out Martha. 'What type of nut is used to flavour a traditional Bakewell tart?'

'Ooh, that's a tricky one,' says the ghost of Robert, picking up the pen. 'Any ideas?'

'Come on, Mum, you must know this!' cajoles my mother, nudging Nana. 'You used to make Bakewell tarts all the time!'

'Oh go on, Edna, help us out,' smiles Caroline.

Nana, it appears, has her mind on other matters.

'This is my daughter, Gabrielle,' she announces, turning to face me.

There is a stunned silence.

'Granddaughter,' I correct, giving a bark of embarrassed laughter. 'So, Nana, about those nuts—'

'And you'll never guess what she's gone and done,' Nana continues.

By now the whole dining room is listening, all hopes of the quiz abandoned.

'She's given a speech. A televised speech. To the United Nations!'

There is another, even greater stunned silence.

'Nana, what are you talking about?' I hiss.

'It was shown on the telly,' smiles Nana, with real pride in her eyes.

'Goodness, Gabrielle. That's very impressive!' exclaims Caroline.

'Golly, I had no idea you were so clever, well done you!' congratulates Martha from across the room.

'No!' I stammer, feeling myself go as red as ketchup. 'No, honestly, I haven't done anything like that.'

'Don't listen to her, she's just being modest!' Nana bludgeons on.

'Are you getting confused with Gabby's episode of *Hollyoaks*, Mum?' my mother jumps in. 'You know? The one where she was a nurse?'

'No,' replies Nana resolutely.

Thankfully, we are saved by the arrival of dessert.

'You look a bit tired, Mum,' says my mother – a dramatic understatement, since Nana is now fast asleep in a drunken stupor. 'I think I'd better take you back to your room.'

'Do you want me to do that for you, Frances?' offers Martha.

'No, no, I've got it,' smiles Mum, going round the table to Nana's wheelchair.

I should point out that by this point, both myself and my mother have also drunk rather a large amount of wine, in my case simply topping up the excesses of the night before. Nor are we accustomed to the workings of Nana's chair.

'Oof,' puffs Mum, trying to manoeuvre it through the door. 'That's odd, we appear to be stuck.'

That is when we see the problem. Neither of us has realised that we need to secure Nana's footrests in place, and her legs have swung out at about ninety degrees each, causing her to do the splits against the door frame.

One of Martha's sons, Alfie, a rather dashing young man in his early thirties, rushes to our aid and takes control of the wheelchair.

Alas, the debacle merely continues.

Due to her limited mobility and rather robust build (a family feature), Nana needs a hoist to heave her out of her wheelchair and safely into the armchair in her room. Not a regular visitor to the nursing home, Alfie is clearly unaware of this.

'Come on, Edna!' he cries, heaving Nana up UNDER THE ARMPITS and attempting to carry her. Having completely misjudged her weight, he finds himself propelled into the chair with her, and a rather bemused yet thrilled Nana wakes up to discover him sitting on her lap.

By the time we have dispatched a very embarrassed and apologetic Alfie ('FRIGHTFULLY sorry, everyone, absolutely pathetic. Must get myself down the gym, HA HA HA!'), Nana has fallen into a deep doze.

'I just need to pop back and have a chat to Martha,' says Mum, excusing herself from the room.

I sit down carefully on the end of Nana's bed, unfortunately releasing a giant farting sound as the special support mattress deflates beneath me.

'Sorry, Nana,' I whisper.

'I'm not asleep, dear,' she replies, shooting open one eye and bringing out a stash of custard creams.

She looks me up and down.

'Everything all right, is it?' she asks.

Thinking to myself, to hell with it – if you can't open up to a mad person, who can you open up to? – I find myself explaining the horrors of the past few days.

'Mum and Dad have bought me these books, Nana. Books on how to behave properly and be more of a lady. The thing is, I don't want to be more of a lady. I know I drink too much and make a tit of myself, but to be honest, I really enjoy it. I don't want to have early nights and go to the gym and discover a love of kale. I want to go to the pub, drink ten pints and discover how many fags I can fit in my mouth.'

A momentary look of horror flashes across my grand-mother's face.

'That's cigarettes, Nana. Not gay men.'

'Ah,' she replies, cramming another custard cream in her own mouth.

'But the thing is,' I continue, 'I really love Mum and Dad and don't want to keep embarrassing them and have them worrying about me all the time. It isn't fair on them. I'd also really like a boyfriend, but I just seem to repulse everyone I meet. What do you think I should do? Should I try and rein things in a bit?'

Nana looks at me with her kind old eyes and smiles.

'The thing is, dear,' she says, 'when you get to my age, you stop caring what other people think of you. And you really regret all those years you wasted worrying about everyone else's opinion. You're only young once. Just go out and enjoy yourself, that's my advice.'

'Thanks, Nana.' I smile, feeling a lump forming in my throat.

'Live for yourself, dearie, and stop trying to impress everyone else,' she concludes, before cackling, 'UNLESS YOU WANT TO ROGER THEM.'

That evening, I sit down with my parents at the dinner table and apologise for my behaviour the night before.

'You don't need to say sorry, sweetheart,' says my mother, passing me the joint of Quorn. 'We're just worried about you. All Dad and I want is for you to be happy.'

'Yes, and perhaps remember your key next time you go out,' adds my father.

'Yes, very sorry about—'

'Rather than throwing pebbles at our bedroom window at 3 a.m. That double glazing doesn't come cheap, you know.'

'I'm really sorry,' I say again. 'But please don't worry – I'm getting my life back on track. In fact, I've actually started dating someone.'

'Really?' my mum gasps, nearly knocking her wine glass over in shock.

'Yes!' I flagrantly fib. 'A really nice boy. Steady job. Good head of hair. You'll probably meet him at the wedding.'

'Well, that's wonderful news, darling, absolutely fabulous!' beams my mother, looking genuinely thrilled.

'Good for you!' chimes in my father, also beaming. 'I hope he's good enough for our Gabby.'

Well, I think I can say with some certainty, Father, that he ISN'T good enough for your Gabby. Mainly due to the fact that he doesn't actually exist.

Shit, I think to myself that night as I climb wearily into bed. There's nothing for it. I have precisely eight months to find myself a man to take to the wedding.

Suddenly, I hit a brainwave. I'm calling Edward.

It is here that I must share with you some very sad news about my dear Nana. Since I wrote this chapter she has unfortunately, um, DIED, and it is an event that I cannot help but feel partly responsible for.

My latest hideous part-time job venture involved working at my local delicatessen. Having given myself RSI from six hours a day slavishly working the ham slicer and had my wages docked for accidentally leaving the outdoor heater on all night, I was not enjoying the job at all. Matters were made worse by the fact that I'd agreed to work weekends. Arranging blocks of stinking bishop cheese and large chorizo sausages at 7 a.m., while riding the waves of a tequila-induced hangover, is not a pleasant experience.

So one weekend, having been invited to a house party that would no doubt leave me still paralytic by morning and sitting somewhere with a traffic cone on my head, I decided to tell a little white lie. I rang my mother immediately afterwards.

'Is it really, really awful to pretend that Nana has died and that I need to go to her funeral on Saturday?' I asked.

Mum was surprisingly okay about it.

'Don't be silly, it's fine!' she reassured me. 'Your grand-mother is as strong as an ox. She's got years left in her.'

And so, with a reasonably clear conscience, I trotted off to the party, where I did indeed get absolutely poleaxed and found myself trying to cook pasta in the toaster at 4 a.m.

On Monday morning, I received the call.

'Now you're not to blame yourself . . .' my mother began.

My stomach dropped.

'Unfortunately, Nana HAS died,' she continued. 'But she was very old and went very peacefully. Nobody could have seen it coming.'

Oh my God. I had CURSED her.

My family have never let me forget it, in a jokey 'remember the time when you killed Nana?' way. Not helped by the fact

that I couldn't get time off work for the funeral, since in the
eyes of my employer it had ALREADY BLOODY HAPPENED.

Sorry, Nana. I'm pretty sure that you of all people would
have found the whole thing very funny.

Not Dating Material

Two years ago, I spent the summer at the Edinburgh Fringe Festival. I say *Fringe* Festival, but so much of the four weeks I was there was spent whoring around that it should really be called the Edinburgh Minge Festival.

I was working on the street team at one of the largest

venues. This meant being in charge of flyering and promot-
ing a selection of shows, in return for free accommodation
and pocket money for the duration of the festival. I couldn't
believe the glittering, exciting world I had been thrust into.
Actors, comedians, dancers and storytellers all mixed together
for what seemed to be a month-long bender, performing
every day and letting loose every night, high on adrenaline
and the success of their sold-out shows. Or just high.

For me, those four weeks were spent doing some half-
hearted flyering in the daytime (a lot of the flyers would, by
freak accident, blow themselves into the bin) before kicking
up my heels, knocking back eight pints of Ginger Grouse
and shamelessly throwing myself into the path of every
famous comedian I laid eyes on. Although I didn't manage
to pull anyone A-list, B-list or even ON the list (in the end
I gave up and shagged the lighting boy who worked at the
Underbelly), I had a bloody good time trying and made some
friends for life.

It was during those weeks that I met Edward. Edward was
the cousin of one of my fellow street team members, and now
firm friend, Jessa. It was clear from the start that he didn't
really feel at peace during his week-long stay at the festival.
Coming from Cambridge University, where I gather he was
something of a big shot, he had found himself thrust into an
environment where he was neither known nor recognised,
surrounded by real celebrities who would not talk to him and
VIP bars that he wasn't allowed entry to.

I, for one, could not stand the boy. Forced to spend several evenings with him, I ground my teeth as he loudly complained through the comedy shows and rolled his eyes at the cabaret acts. He also, come rain or shine, insisted on wearing a ridiculous pair of Hawaiian-print flip-flops, as if we were not in freezing cold Scotland but on a budget holiday in Marbella. Perhaps it was my complete (admittedly freakishly rare) lack of interest in him, or the fact that I loudly and drunkenly answered him back and gave as good as I got, but he took something of a shine to me.

'Edward really likes you,' Jessa told me one evening as we were heading out to Hobos, the dingiest club in the whole of Edinburgh. 'He's got a heart of gold, really. He's just used to these stuck-up, pretentious girls at Cambridge and needs someone really down-to-earth to bring him out of his shell.'

'I hardly think he needs bringing out of his shell, the bloody ... the bloody BRAGGART,' I spluttered, letting out a small Ginger Grouse-based belch. 'I've never met a more outspoken person in my life. And I grew up in Wales.'

Unexpectedly, though, I found myself warming to Edward that night. After a few more drinks, I was soon beside myself with laughter at his 1970s dance moves and the way his flip-flops kept getting stuck to the floor, causing him to step out of them. Soon I had robot-walked my way over to him until we were dancing nose to nose, grinning stupidly at one another and only occasionally breaking away to throw out a disco finger. And that was when it happened.

I don't know what it is about me, but people seem to RELISH picking me up – literally – on dance floors. Now, make no mistake, I am not a waif-like girl. I am built like a brick shithouse. But for some unfathomable reason, people always seem to drastically underestimate just how heavy I will actually be.

The worst instance of this occurred on a night out in London with Katie. We were, at the time, in the habit of going to a club called the Roxy – an establishment where everyone is between the ages of eighteen and twenty, making me, at the tender age of twenty-three, the Old Woman of the Hills. Amazingly, I seemed to be quite a hit with the young men and was in no way short of people to dance with. (I can't help thinking that I was something of a novelty to them. Like a child dancing with its grandparent at a wedding. In fact, I'm surprised the young men didn't ask to stand on top of my feet while I gaily whirled them around the dance floor.) Anyway, one night in the Roxy, while dancing with a young whippersnapper to One Direction, he suddenly reached out and touched my face, singing (in no way ironically), 'You don't know you're beautiful'. This is where the horror should have ended.

Unfortunately, he then, without warning, decided to pick me up and swing me round. He managed to get me about two inches off the floor, but then buckled like a collapsible garden chair, falling to the ground and screaming in pain: 'My back! My back!'

Immediately, everyone formed a circle round him and the DJ was given the signal to put the main lights on.

'Who did this to you?' the bouncer asked, looking around

for the rogue attacker, as I slowly slunk backwards, desperately trying not to draw attention to myself.

At that moment Katie came out of the toilets, surveyed the scene in horror ('Gabs, what the hell have you done?') and we did a runner out the door.

Anyway, that night in Hobos, Edward also decided to pick me up under the armpits. Panicking, I swung my legs round his waist, causing him to stagger backwards and crash to the floor, bringing about five people down with us.

We were swiftly ejected from the club and tottered out arm in arm, flagging down the nearest rickshaw, which Edward very sweetly directed to the only joint still serving pizza at 1 a.m., all the way on the other side of Edinburgh. We didn't snog. Instead, like the perfect gentleman I now saw him as, he paid the rickshaw to drop me off at my residence, while he walked himself home.

The Fringe ended and we went our separate ways – him back to being the darling of Cambridge and me back to being the dunce of drama school. But something had been stirred within me. I never forgot pompous Edward. And because I became good friends with Jessa, I had plenty of opportunities to see him again. Though of course, as sod's law would have it, as soon as I began to have feelings for him, he completely lost all shred of interest in me.

Most people would leave it there. Resign themselves to the fact that this was never going to be a thing and move on with their lives. Being mentally unstable, however, I devised a plan that I was convinced would soon have Edward crazed with lust, sweating and churning with desire: I would shag all of his friends.

I realise how ludicrous it sounds. But it was a good idea in theory. I somehow thought that if Edward could see me getting off with his mates, and hear how great it had been, then it might conjure up a bit of the old green-eyed monster and subsequently rekindle those feelings he had once had for me.

As I say . . . it was a good idea in theory.

As it turned out, meeting Edward's friends was a piece of cake. He conveniently threw a house-warming party at his new flat in east London, and I tagged along with Jessa. Edward, who I suspect was not entirely thrilled to see me, ignored me all night. And I triumphantly left with two phone numbers: that of Jason, one of Edward's childhood friends, and Kenneth, a boy from his university course.

Jason was so smooth, dark and good-looking that he gave off the air of a pantomime villain. Our date was booked at a posh Japanese restaurant in Kensington, which I had great trouble finding, with Google Maps leading me to the entrance of a dog-grooming parlour. (I am not quite as bad a map-reader as my mother, who on a road trip round central Spain with my father once remarked, 'Isn't it weird how the road we are on is so straight, yet on the map it's all blue and wiggly?' before realising that she was following a river.)

Jason was waiting for me at the door when I arrived, with a suit slung over his arm that he had just picked up from the dry-cleaner's. This in itself blew me away. I do not know anyone my age who can afford to take their clothes to the dry-cleaner's. The sum total of my 'dry-cleaning' amounts to me, ten minutes before work, angrily ramming an iron over my shirt, placed on a towel on the floor. (The ironing board is sadly no longer usable since I drunkenly sat on it one night and severely bent the legs.) We were then ushered to a table, whereupon Jason asked me what I would like to drink.

'Red wine, please!' I declared confidently.

'One red wine and a bottle of still water, please,' he told the waiter.

'What . . . you're not drinking?' I asked, alarm bells already ringing.

'No, but don't let me stop you.' He smiled, making me feel less sexy young thing and more greedy old wino.

We sat staring at one another.

I've never been very good with pauses in conversations. I become so awkward that I start gibbering complete drivel in a desperate attempt to fill the silence. Once, with Robyn, there was what she has since described as a 'companionable silence' while we both sat smoking cigarettes. I, on the other hand, interpreted it as a 'hideously awkward silence', managing to last for three whole seconds before bursting out with 'Have you seen that fresh new tarmac that's been laid outside?'

As the waiter placed a large glass of red in front of me, and Jason slowly poured out two glasses of water, I could feel the familiar awkward tension rising.

WHY IS NOBODY SAYING ANYTHING?

Finally, unable to take it any longer, I unfolded my napkin from the table and tied it round my head.

'Want to see my impression of Mother Teresa?' I asked. He did not.

Luckily, our tiny portions of sushi were eaten fairly quickly, as I knocked back the wine on a near-empty stomach, still reeling from the humiliation of my Mother Teresa gaffe. Excusing myself to go the loo, I stared in horror at my flushed, sweating reflection in the mirror and hastily slapped some powder on, which unfortunately mixed with the sweat on my face to form a paste.

Calm down, Gabrielle, I told myself, smearing it off with a tissue. You need to calm down.

By the time I emerged, Jason had already discreetly paid the bill and was standing with my coat over his arm, along with his dry-cleaning.

'I don't suppose you fancy a drink round mine?' he asked.

This did strike me as slightly odd, seeing as Jason was not drinking, but I had by this point drunk enough for the both of us and was so relieved that I hadn't completely and utterly blown it that I found myself enthusiastically agreeing.

'Can we walk, or do we need to get the tube?' I asked.

He laughed, pointing a key fob at the flashiest sports car I have ever seen in my life, which beeped and lit up, inviting us inside. Shit. Clearly Jason was absolutely fucking loaded.

As we drove along (Jason's fast and flashy driving rather hindered by the number of speed bumps and traffic lights we encountered), I couldn't help but think back to that journey with Edward, going at about five miles an hour in a rickshaw, clutching two pepperoni pizzas and screaming with drunken laughter, and how much nicer it had been.

Once we were inside the flat (which turned out to be a swanky bachelor pad with not only a large double bedroom but an actual spare room), we somewhat unsurprisingly got down to business.

It wasn't until three days afterwards, when Jason still had not texted, that I rang Jessa up and confessed to what had happened.

'Oh GOD, you didn't sleep with Jason Matthews, did you? He's the biggest rake around. He fucks and chucks girls, that's what he does.'

I had no idea if this was actually true, but I felt used.

My date with Kenneth was about ten times worse.

While Jason was all shmoozy, confident and cunning as a fox, Kenneth was sweet, fumbling and bumbling as a drunken panda. We arranged to meet near his flat – not at a sleek restaurant this time, but in a quiet and cosy pub.

It was clear from the outset that Kenneth was extremely nervous.

'Hello!' he cried, jumping up and knocking his knee hard on the table, which he pretended not to notice.

Obviously unsure whether to go for a kiss on the cheek, a hug or a handshake, he ended up sort of clasping my shoulders and shaking them, while tears of pain shone in his eyes.

'Would you, I mean how are, shall I get us some drinks?' he gibbered.

'That would be great.' I smiled in the most reassuring manner I could manage. 'I'll have a gin and tonic, please.'

'Single or double?' he asked.

Aaagh. I have never in my life ordered myself a single at the bar. For me, it is pointless. A complete waste of money. It takes about twenty of the things to get me drunk, by which point I am so bloated with tonic water that I need to go home and deflate quietly on the toilet. Yet when a man offers to buy me a drink, I feel greedy and frivolous asking for a double measure. Or a large glass of wine.

The same goes for the speed at which I drink. As you have probably gathered by now, I have a frighteningly high alcohol tolerance and can whittle my way through a bottle of wine like a camel consuming water. I'll be nearly two thirds of the way down my glass, ready to go up and order another, while my date, the FULLY GROWN MAN, will only have managed to take a teeny-tiny, waspish sip from his own. I then find myself staring at him resentfully, willing him to stop talking and drink faster, while I toy with the tiny, sorry splash at the bottom of my glass. Much better, surely, to each be in charge of our own drinks for the evening, meaning that both parties, be it due to tolerance or budget, can go at the pace that suits them.

'Here we are!' said Kenneth, shakily placing down a gin and tonic and a beer.

Conversation was extremely stilted. Desperate not to lap him by a whole glass, I took the tiniest sips of my drink possible, asking him about his family back in Northern Ireland

and his plans to become a journalist. He managed to ask me a few things about myself but I could tell he was not really listening to the replies, instead nervously nodding like the Churchill dog and adjusting his shirt.

In fact, Kenneth and I were so glaringly two people on a first date that soon people had started nudging one another and smiling fondly in our direction.

'I'm really glad you agreed to meet me,' Kenneth said, shuffling round the booth so that we were side by side.

'Um, yes!' I said, edging a bit to my right, causing him to shuffle along again and join me. Good God, this was like a bedroom farce. Any minute now I would fall off the end of the seat.

'It's good to see you again.' I smiled.

'Yes, good to see you again,' he repeated. Then, with all the subtlety of a sledgehammer, he stretched out a long, lanky arm and put it around my shoulders. This was made worse by the fact that I had by this point managed to lean my body about eight inches away from him, giving his arm an extremely extended, comic effect. It was like being propositioned by Mr Tickle. I noticed the people sitting at the bar nudging each other again and giggling in our direction.

'Just popping to the loo,' I said, draining the last of my drink.

Oh God help, I texted Robyn from the cubicle.

How's it going?!! she replied.

Not good. Don't fancy him at all. He's got arms like eels.

Hahahaha.

Nothing for it. Going to have to get us both drunk.

Taking the situation into my own hands, I arrived back at our table with double gin and tonics for the both of us, along with two Jägerbombs.

'Right, bottoms up!' I cried.

It soon became clear to me what a grave, grave mistake this was. Half an hour later, the poor boy was completely and utterly mullered.

'You've got amazing eyes,' he slurred at me, before leaning in for a kiss.

Even more mortifying than the kiss was the fact that the other pub customers, having been emotionally invested in our date from the start, all gave a big cheer and started clapping.

'Ha ha!' I laughed nervously, giving him a quick peck and pulling away.

It was then that I noticed Kenneth's eyes were not open.

'Hey,' I said, looking down and jiggling my shoulder, where his head was now lolling. 'HEY!'

Oh my God. He was asleep.

In some hideous role reversal, I then found myself slinging Kenneth's eel-like arm back over my shoulder and manhandling him up the road to his flat before resignedly catching the tube home.

Needless to say, the plan had failed, and I found myself no closer to seeing Edward's rubber flip-flops slung across my bedroom floor, as I so badly desired.

Tonight, however ... ALL THAT IS GOING TO CHANGE!

It's a freezing cold January evening, yet I am dolled up to

the nines and about to head to Brixton to meet Jessa, Edward and one of Edward's friends, who I am determined shan't be shagged.

Edward is clearly completely unaware of my fruitless pursuit of two of his closest mates (which I now see as something of a blessing), and amazingly, we once again hit it off and are soon drunkenly snogging on the club dance floor. I mean, I *think* we have hit it off. I can't help but worry that Edward has simply resigned himself to the fact that we are going to be having sex tonight, in the manner of 'let's get it over and done with and then maybe she'll leave me alone'. But beggars can't be choosers, and I'm rolling with it.

Several hours later, and just as I had planned, we are falling through the door of Edward's flat.

'Everyone's asleep . . . You need to be quiet,' he tells me, putting a finger to his lips and turning round to lock the door.

'As quiet as a mouse . . . SQUEAK!' I giggle, before doing over-the-top pantomime 'quiet walking', unfortunately missing the third step on the staircase and sliding down with a crash.

Hastily Edward hustles me into his bedroom and shuts the door.

After a brief pause, where we sort of stare at one another like two cage-fighters waiting for the bell, I take matters into my own hands and lunge in for a kiss.

'Hmm, what have we here?' I murmur, attempting to undo Edward's belt.

'Just going to the loo for a sec,' he says suddenly,

extracting himself and heading to the bathroom, I presume to collect condoms or inspect his pubic hair before the big event.

It is then that I come up with what seems like a brilliant idea. I am yet to learn that men do not generally enjoy physical comedy in the bedroom. In a man's eyes, it is not particularly sexy for a girl to strip down to her bra, pants and a pair of suspenders, then when his back is turned pop on a red clown's nose. Or, when she has just given him a blowjob and is asked how he tastes, for her to smack her lips and reply, 'My compliments to the chef!'

Yet in my drunken state, I decide to try it again.

Hearing Edward still rustling around in the bathroom, I whip off all my clothes with lightning speed and lie stark bollock naked on his landing, my head propped up by one arm and legs seductively crossed.

After what feels like a lifetime, Edward opens the bathroom door and stares at me in shock.

'PAINT ME LIKE ONE OF YOUR FRENCH GIRLS, JACK!' I bellow, bursting into laughter.

It does not go down as well as I might have hoped.

'Gabby, what the fuck?' Edward whispers, looking less aroused and more extremely pissed off. 'Get up, I've got housemates!'

I'm once again ushered into his room like a naughty child, whereupon he firmly shuts the door and puts the bolt across, as if worried that I'm about to streak naked through the house and take a dump on a housemate's bed.

'Sorry,' I mutter. 'Thought it would be funny.'

We get down to it then.

Now I know that first times are always a disappointment. Too much anticipation has built up, each party too worried about their own performance to really let loose and enjoy themselves. But in the history of bad first times, I think this is possibly the worst.

I flail around beneath Edward for a bit before deciding to take matters into my own hands by climbing on top of him (just about managing not to cry out 'YEE HA!' and mime a lasso). The problem is, we are in totally different rhythms. Bouncing around like a drunk riding a Shetland pony, I notice Edward wince several times as I land painfully and inelegantly on his cock. In fact, so out of rhythm are we that I am starting to feel a bit seasick.

'This is fantastic!' I cry, trying not to projectile-vomit on to the wall behind him.

'It is . . . it's great!' he replies, his face contorted in pain.

Eventually we decide that enough is enough. I can't believe it. Months and months of yearning, planning and scheming culminate in me announcing, 'We'll bang in the morning,' rolling off him and falling into an exhausted sleep.

Things are decidedly awkward the next morning. Not just because Edward screams and slaps my thigh, mistaking my false eyelashes for a huge spider, but also because I think we both realise that whatever attraction we had for one another died a death during last night's drunken romp.

I make my escape, and as I stagger down the street in last

night's clothes, feeling the eyes of the whole of Brixton on me, I take out my phone and call Danny.

Since my unceremonious firing from the call centre, Danny has remained one of my closest and most special friends. Being a fellow writer/actor, he has a similarly haphazard schedule, and as he lives only a few streets away from me, we are often able to slope off to our local pub on a midweek lunchtime and get absolutely bladdered together.

As a man who loves men, Danny has an unparalleled knowledge of the male mind, particularly regarding sex and relationships. He has therefore become my wise counsellor, like a rather more outrageous version of Grandmother Willow from *Pocahontas*.

Rather than go into the horrors of last night over the phone, I ask if he'll meet me at our usual pub for lunch. When I arrive, I can see him sitting outside in the smoking area, two pints and his head on the table.

'Oh God,' he groans, looking up as I sit down. 'Oh God, oh God, oh God.'

This is the great thing about Danny. Whenever I have done anything shameful or regrettable, he can always be relied upon to top it tenfold.

'What have you done?' I ask, feeling the first waves of hysteria rising already. Please God, let it involve a Grindr hook-up.

'I ended up at that Italian man's house last night. You know, the one I met on Grindr.'

'Oh, right.' I nod, calmly. Yes, YES!!

With barely contained elation, I light a cigarette, sit back and wait for the tale to unfold.

'He seemed a nice enough guy,' Danny begins. 'Big dick – eight inches and thick.'

Having observed Danny on Grindr several times, I am constantly amazed and envious at the ease with which gay men arrange sex. They are completely upfront and honest from the start about what they want from the night and what they have to offer. Speaking in a special coded language, they will in a few succinct messages establish whether the other is a top or a bottom, the size of their penis (often including a photo) and whereabouts they are based.

It is a stark and refreshing contrast to the cloak-and-dagger nonsense us straight people insist on putting ourselves through – all nudge, nudge, wink, wink, let's pretend we're just meeting for civilised drinks when really I intend to come back to your flat within the hour and give you a DAMN GOOD PORKING.

'So you went over to his?' I ask.

'Yeah. Problem was, there was a bit of a language barrier. The guy barely spoke a word of English.'

Oh God, this is going to be good, I think to myself, settling down as a child might for an (admittedly slightly more sordid) episode of *Watch with Mother*.

'One word he did seem to know, though, was "opera". So there I am, horny as fuck, making small talk about *La Bohème*, neither of us having a clue as to what the other was saying. Anyway, I managed to make out that he's been to some opera house in Italy, so before he started banging on about that, I jumped in and asked him, "What makes you hard?"'

I grin. 'Straight to the point.'

'Exactly. Except he couldn't understand what I was asking him. Kept repeating, "What, what?" "WHAT. MAKES. YOU. HARD?" I said again, but he still wasn't getting it. I mean, Jesus Christ, what did he think I came over for? A cup of tea? He'd been VERY clear on Grindr about what he wanted, if you know what I mean. So in the end, I grabbed his laptop, paused *La Bohème* and went on to Google Translate.'

'You didn't.'

'Yes. Needs must, I'm afraid. But when I typed in "What makes you hard?" and the computer blasts out the translation in Italian, the guy frowns at me and says, "'What makes me difficult?"'

I splutter with laughter into my pint.

'Anyway, after a bit of jumbled explanation, mime, charades, et cetera, we finally got down to it. But having gone through all that palaver, we were both pretty exhausted and he couldn't get it up. Eventually, though, as we were lying down taking a breather, I felt him, you know, enter me.'

'He finally got it up!' I cheer.

'Yes, that's what I thought. AT LAST! I said to myself. But then I turn around and . . . You won't believe this, Gabs.'

'What, what?!'

'He's rogering me with a twelve-inch pink dildo.'

After I've cried with laughter and gone to get us two more pints, conversation turns to my evening with Edward.

'Surely you feel better now?' Danny asks, once I've related the sorry tale. 'Having finally achieved the conquest?'

'No,' I find myself replying truthfully. 'I feel embarrassed. And a bit cheap.'

This very frank admission startles us both and hangs in the air for several minutes. Feeling myself slowly turning red, I stick my head under the table and pretend to be rummaging around in my bag for some filters.

When I look up, Danny is watching me sort of sadly and fondly.

'You need cheering up,' he says. 'Fancy coming out in Soho with me tonight?'

'Definitely not.'

'Go on.'

'No.'

And so precisely eight hours later, I find myself in Freedom Bar, swinging wildly round a metal pole.

'Fuck that fucker!' I yell happily to Danny as he comes over with two more large gin and tonics. 'I am young, single and ready to mingle. Or fat, single and ready for a Pringle! Ha ha ha.'

Danny is never short of male attention and is soon batting off a crowd of ogling men, like bees round a honey pot.

'Wheeeee!!!' I cry, swinging myself with dangerous speed around the pole and nearly bending the thing in half.

By 1 a.m., I am once again absolutely plastered. Looking across at Danny, I can safely say that he is in pretty much the same state.

'Gabs, I'm gonna go,' he slurs to me.

I look behind him to where a small, good-looking young guy is waiting. A twink, as they say in the gay world.

'OH YES?' I ask, winking heavily in the manner of Dame Edna.

'Will you be all right getting home?' Danny asks.

'Yes, yes, fine and dandy. I'm just gonna have a bit of a dance, then I'll leave.'

I really do mean to go home. But while standing in the smoking area having what I think will be my final cigarette of the night, I meet a young man named Sven.

I say 'Sven' optimistically – I am so drunk that I don't quite hear it properly, but nonetheless I confidently call him this for the remainder of the evening. Sven is Swedish and visiting London with a group of friends. Faced with this mad-eyed drunken Londoner, I think he sees me as something of a tourist attraction and therefore decides to leave his friends and spend the remainder of the evening with me.

'Wow ... you're wild,' he notes with admiration in his voice as I knock back the last of my gin.

'What was that, Sven? Oh yes, quite wild indeed.'

'Do you fancy going someplace else?' he asks.

For someone who is not a resident here, Sven seems to have an encyclopedic knowledge of London, leading us through numerous little back streets until we arrive at another bar.

Goodness ... this is not my usual cheap sort of place. A line of suited bouncers flanks the door, while a pair of curtains hides the inside of the venue from view. Sven has what seems to be an in-depth whispered discussion with one of the men on the door before handing over a staggeringly large wad of cash and ushering me inside.

I gaze around. Oh my God.

We are in a strip club.

Everywhere I look there are scantily clad women wearing nothing but skimpy G-strings and nipple tassels; gyrating on the stage, sitting on people's laps or carrying trays of drinks.

'Do you like women?' Sven asks me.

I really don't know what comes over me. Perhaps it's the humiliation of my night with Edward, my utter failure so far to find a date for the wedding, or just the gallon of alcohol inside me, but I suddenly find myself feeling extremely care-free and reckless.

'Oh yes, very much so,' I reply, smiling serenely.

'Which one would you like?' Sven asks.

Oh God.

Before I know it, about ten women are lined up before me, smiling and winking and sticking their chests out as if this is a Miss World contest and I am the balding male judge.

'I'll have that one,' I say, pointing to the least threatening of the ten.

Sven has a word with another large, terrifying-looking bouncer, who gestures to the girl and then leads us over to a PRIVATE BOOTH.

Oh my God. A private booth?! What the hell are we going to be doing in there?

'Could you bring me a large gin and tonic, please?' I ask a nearby naked waitress.

We enter the booth and the thick, velvety curtains are pulled around us, sealing us in.

'Hi, my name is Crystal,' smiles my chosen lady. 'Can my friend come in too? We're training her up.'

'BRING IN THE FRIEND!' I declare magnanimously, hoping that the more of us there are crowded in here, the less awkward it will be. Less seedy striptease, more cheese and wine party, perhaps.

'So . . . you like girls?' smiles Crystal, sashaying towards me.

So here's the thing. I love women in all their shapes and forms. But sadly, I am a sucker for penis (if you'll excuse the expression) and have never been attracted to a girl in that way. As a consequence, I am starting to find this whole scenario distinctly awkward.

'Sit down, Crystal!' I cry, slapping the cushion beside me heartily.

Looking slightly bemused, Crystal does what I ask.

'Now, tell me about yourself,' I begin. 'How long have you worked here? Is the pay good?'

Having twigged that I am in no way attracted her, and with Honey and Sven seemingly getting on famously, Crystal proceeds to order a bottle of Prosecco and the two of us have an in-depth heart-to-heart about working conditions, the cost of rent and the best place to shop for nipple tassels.

Twenty minutes later, absolutely plastered and having a wonderful time, I look round and beam at Sven.

'All right over there?' I shout.

'Here,' slurs back Sven, handing me his wallet.

It is then I realise that Honey is preparing to do some sort of erotic dance for us – standing in the centre of the booth and gyrating around with a series of crotch thrusts, hip wiggles and leg strokes.

'Oh, bravo!!' I clap. 'VERY good indeed, Honey!'

I reach into Sven's wallet to find some form of note to tuck into Honey's thong, as I have seen done in the movies. Unfortunately, however, I am so absolutely blotto by this point that I can't quite see what I'm doing. This results in Honey having all sorts posted into her underwear – rail tickets, receipts and quite possibly even a library card.

Eventually our booth session comes to an end. Feeling the first horrible twinges of sobriety overtaking me, I bid farewell to Sven (promising to call him if I'm ever in Sweden) and stagger out of the club into the chilly, unforgiving 5 a.m. light.

Hopping into the safety of an Uber, I sit with my head in my hands, wondering how things can have escalated QUITE so drastically in the past forty-eight hours. Wearily, my mind flits back to a line from one of my mother's etiquette books, regarding hosting a dinner party:

Do not dance yourself, when, by doing so, you are preventing a guest from enjoying that pleasure. If invited, say that you do not wish to take the place of a guest upon the floor, and introduce the gentleman who invites you to some lady friend who dances.

Pretty much the same as strip clubs, then.

10

Hen ~~Do~~ Don't

Two fruitless months have somehow passed since the trauma of my night of passion/seasickness with Edward. I am very aware that time is running out for me to find my dream man (or frankly ANY man) to take to the wedding – so far the most interest anyone has shown in me has come from a lesbian stripper. However, I am excited to be heading back to Cardiff for Emma's hen do. Starved of a good old Welsh knees-up, I cannot wait to put on my eight layers of slap and hit the town. (The Ibiza trip, I am relieved to announce, has proved impossible to organise, even with Natasha at the helm.)

A night out in Cardiff is a very different experience to a night out in London. London is self-consciously cool and follows the rule of 'less is more'. No need to get glammed up – jeans, nice top and a jacket will do. Heels are swapped for designer trainers. Make-up is clean-faced and natural-looking, despite taking over an hour to apply. Hair is all glossy natural waves, though that is only achievable thanks to a very expensive blow-dry.

Cardiff has no such qualms. Here the rule is 'MORE IS FUCKIN' MORE, YA PUSSIES!' If we've made an effort, we're going to bloody well show it.

Tits. Legs. Tan.

Coats and jackets are for utter drips: the clubs here have no cloakrooms, meaning you'd either have to hang your coat over your arm all night or bundle it into a corner somewhere on the dance floor, only for it to be tripped over and puked on later in the evening. Fake eyelashes, or 'boy entrancers', as they have become known, are an absolute must. Several of my friends will often layer up their false eyelashes, wearing two or three pairs at once for maximum impact. (Unfortunately this results in eyelids so top-heavy that it's hard to keep them open. And God forbid you should fall asleep in your false eyelashes, as Emma once discovered when she awoke one morning with both her eyes sealed shut.)

Heels are also a complete necessity. What sort of sick weirdo would wear flat shoes on a night out? The formula is simple: the higher the heel, the longer and thinner your legs will look in your unforgiving bodycon dress. Skyscraper stilettos are teetered around on at the start of the night, before eventually being whipped off and slung over the shoulder, meaning that the entire female population of Cardiff is tiptoeing around the streets barefoot, avoiding shards of glass, mashed-up chips and puddles of sick.

The logistics of the night are completely different too.

In London, there is Uber, which makes getting from your flat to the club an absolute doddle. At the click of a button, a Toyota Prius will almost immediately pull up outside, causing a mad panic in which glasses of wine are downed, cigarettes are chugged away on and nobody can find their keys. You will then all sit in painful silence for the entire journey, terrified that the slightest disturbance might affect your 4.2-star rating.

In Cardiff, there is no such thing as Uber and all taxis need to be booked about a year in advance. Make the perilous decision of booking on the night and often three or four different cab firms will need to be rung before you eventually get through to a pissed-off-sounding coordinator. She will then ask which village you need picking up from and inform you that the next taxi won't be available for another two hours.

This leaves you plenty of time to get absolutely shit-faced on Echo Falls, before all piling into the taxi at 9 p.m., armed with various bottles to sustain you for the hour-long drive. The taxi journey itself will often be as raucous as the club you're heading to, as everyone sings along to Kiss FM, takes selfies and throws up into their handbags. The taxi driver will be absolutely loving it, turning in his seat at the traffic lights with a cry of 'WHERE ARE WE OFF TO TONIGHT THEN, DARLINGS?' before handing out his number for you to book him to take you home at 2 a.m.

Once in Cardiff, you will bump into literally every single person you know under the age of thirty-five, as the screaming, shrieking throng moves from club to club. No entry fee means you can literally stick your head in, assess the talent and if it's not to your fancy, move on.

There will often be a hefty snaking queue for the best clubs, but this is an experience in itself. In London, the queue is an intimidating, solemn business. Everyone quietly stays in line, shivering in their puffa jackets, before finally getting to the door and being faced by the Spanish Inquisition – huge Mafia-style bouncers shining torches into your handbag, your eyes and up your arse before giving you the most intense frisking of your life and demanding a ten-pound entry fee.

In Cardiff, the queue is a more sociable affair. Looking ahead and behind, you can assess the lads coming in and work out between yourselves which ones you're going to get off with. Best friends are made, along with bitter enemies – often there will be screaming catfights if someone pushes ahead in the queue. Bottles are glugged from, while girls crouch behind parked cars to have a piss, their friends screaming in horror as the steaming trail of urine takes a sharp U-turn and heads towards them.

Finally, there is the issue of alcohol. In London you can expect to pay upwards of ten pounds for some arty-farty cocktail, often set on fire or with a sorry lump of passion fruit floating in it, which you will finish in three sips before spending the next half-hour trying to catch the attention of the surly barman again.

In Cardiff, drinks are cheap and cheerful. Ten pounds will get you a tray of ten vodka shots (perfectly acceptable for one person to drink in one go to a crescendo of whoops/cheers/ table-drumming, before crashing through the door of the ladies' toilets and projectile-vomiting over the hand dryer) or four large glasses of cheap white wine, which you will proceed to take on to the dance floor and slosh over everyone around you.

Given my extensive experience, I feel that arranging a hen do is an area I could truly excel in, so I am irritated yet somewhat unsurprised when Natasha insists on organising the whole thing herself. She does, however, have one task for me.

Hey Gabs! she texts a couple of weeks beforehand. *So I know you wanted to help plan Em's Cardiff do and I've got a job that you'd be perfect for!! Could you book the stripper for the night? None of us girlies have a clue where to look! Xx* This is followed by that bloody emoji of a monkey with its hands over its eyes – one I find that all irritating people are particularly drawn to.

The insult here is so apparent that I nearly text back saying *Sure thing! Let me just have a look through my little black book of masochists, sugar daddies, lady boys and gigolos and select a few personal favourites* but decide against it in case word gets back to my parents, giving them organ failure.

Instead, I decide to rise to the challenge. If Emma wants a stripper . . . BY GUM, IS SHE GETTING A STRIPPER!

I assumed this would be a simple and enjoyable task, imagining myself flipping casually through a glossy catalogue (entitled something like *Pork Sword*, May edition), comparing photos of ripped men dressed as firefighters, policemen and perhaps something more unusual, like a scantily clad orthodontist or a well-hung fishmonger, then pointing to the one I wanted: 'I'll have the sexy tin man pouring oil over himself, please!'

However, it turns out that this is very much not the case.

Denied a catalogue, I find myself on various dubious-looking websites, where I can select my preferred 'dreamboy' and then be put in contact with him directly. The whole thing feels a little underhand and shady. I actually end up texting a couple of the men (who all have extremely normal names, such as Paul and Boris, rather than DONG Juan or Long SHLONG Silver, like I had imagined), asking if they would be prepared to perform in a club in Cardiff.

Both text back very politely, saying they would love to but unfortunately none of the clubs in Cardiff will actually let them in.

I have been brainwashed by films and television programmes, where a stripper taps the shoulder of a girl in the bar and pretends to arrest her, before tossing his helmet aside, whipping off his Velcroed trousers and preparing to squirt whipped cream over his cock. In real life, however, getting a stripper to perform in a club is about as easy as extracting blood from a stone.

Having failed to gain permission from every single club and bar in the whole of south Wales, I resort to actually contacting the five-star hotel that we will be staying in for the night, asking whether they will allow a stripper to perform in the foyer while I beatbox in the background. (Smuggling him into one of our bedrooms feels too sleazy even by my standards.) The answer is an unsurprising no.

And so, with absolute misery, I admit defeat. Natasha makes a big show of being hugely disappointed by this – *I expected more from you, Gabs* – but I know she is secretly thrilled that I am the one to have let Emma down.

The hotel Natasha has booked us into is an extremely classy establishment. Situated in Cardiff Bay, it boasts an award-winning marine spa, in which we will be spending the afternoon before having a slap-up lunch and getting ready for the evening ahead.

Unbeknown to me, it turns out that Emma's mother Jane and her two friends will also be joining us, not just for the spa day but for the night out clubbing as well. I've known Jane since I was three years old and am extremely fond of her . . . but it must be said that she is an almighty party pooper. I'll never forget the time Emma smuggled a bottle of white wine to my house, stolen from her mum's wine cellar, only to crack it open and discover it was alcohol-free.

'Don't,' hisses Emma when we meet in the hotel foyer. 'She insisted on coming. I warned her that she wouldn't like the clubs, but she said she and her girlfriends wanted to shake a tail feather.'

Good grief.

'Coming through, girlies, coming through,' shrieks Natasha, pushing her way in with an extremely large suitcase. I notice Louise wince in pain as the wheels run over her left foot.

'I've booked three rooms,' Natasha declares loudly to the man behind the reception desk.

'Name, please, madam?'

'Natasha.'

'And your surname?'

'Jones,' she replies, rolling her eyes at the audacity of the man.

'We don't seem to have any reservations for Jones here, madam. Do you have your booking reference to hand?'

We all look at one another, stunned. Surely not. Surely Natasha would not have made such a gigantic balls-up as to not book the rooms.

'I wasn't sent a booking reference,' she hisses, looking at the receptionist as if he is insane. 'Or a confirmation email. I just assumed that you had done it.'

'We got a confirmation email!' chimes in Jane, proudly waving a piece of paper in the air.

After a great deal of probing, we finally find Natasha's booking reference hidden amongst the emails on her phone, and realise that she has actually booked the rooms under

Emma's surname. Excited, we head upstairs to change. (Unsurprisingly, Natasha has arranged for her and Emma to share a room, putting me in with Louise. I am secretly relieved by this, having already told one of my mates joining us later that she can crash in my room and sleep in the bath.) Then, dressed in our swimwear, robes and flip-flops, we head down to the restaurant, looking forward to a delicious lunch followed by a relaxing few hours in the spa.

The lunch and spa, it transpires, have most *definitely* not been booked.

'Not to worry, girls.' The hotel manager breezes up to us. 'Our downstairs room is available, so if you don't mind eating on your own, we are going to set up a table for you there.'

Now feeling like utter pillocks in our bikinis and white cotton robes (which insist on untying themselves at any given moment), we awkwardly pile into the lift with the manager and descend to the basement.

Well, it isn't quite what we were expecting.

Having envisaged a cosy lunch in a bustling restaurant, we find ourselves in a gigantic barren conference room. An assortment of desks, chairs and overhead projectors have been pushed to the sides, leaving two trestle tables in the centre, with a tablecloth placed wonkily across. Like a prison interrogation room, the harsh strip lighting blazes down on us, showing up every spot, lump and patch of cellulite on our pale bodies.

We look at one another in horror. I can't deny that I derive a fair amount of pleasure from Natasha's reaction – her face as pinched and angry as a cat's arsehole – as it dawns on her that she's made the second cock-up of the day.

'Well, at least we have lots of room!' I smile, looking down and noticing a huge strip of hair stretching from knee to ankle that I have clearly missed with the razor this morning.

'Yes, and it's nice to have the air con on,' adds Louise through chattering teeth, pulling her thin robe tighter around herself.

One look at Emma's face says it all.

'I need a bloody drink,' she says, plonking herself on one of the plastic office chairs.

The meal itself is served astonishingly quickly, the staff clearly keen to get rid of us and set the room up for a meeting taking place that afternoon. But although everyone makes a heroic effort to keep up a forced air of gaiety, there is no getting around the fact that we have been well and truly ripped off. Half-starved, we attack our small bread rolls before picking at an extremely depressing portion of pasta and chicken.

We quickly polish off the paltry two bottles of wine provided, and I suggest that we order another and just pay for it separately. At this, Jane furrows her brow.

'I think you've had enough now, girls,' she says sternly. 'I don't want you parading around the hotel like a group of drunken lushes.'

Fantastic.

Our trip to the spa turns out to be equally anticlimactic. Thanks to the booking failure, we cannot have any treatments; instead, our passes allow us access to an hour in the rather small, lukewarm swimming pool.

I feel as hairy and pale as a mountain goat, and I try not to look at Natasha as she stretches out her bronzed, toned body on a sunlounger before slowly climbing in and out of the pool an inordinate number of times, clearly seeing herself as the next Halle Berry.

At last it is time for the evening's festivities.

I always feel sorry for the bride on her hen do. One would imagine that in your final hurrah as a single woman, you would want to be looking your absolute best. Instead you must face the humiliation of wearing 'slutty bride paraphernalia': L-plates, devil's horns and anything shaped like a cock – from a 'pin the junk on the hunk' blindfold game, right down to a teeny-tiny pair of dangly penis earrings.

In Emma's case, while the rest of us have dolled ourselves up in our best playsuits and dresses, she is forced to wear a tarty 'bridal gown', complete with a sticky-out tutu that just skims her crotch, and to carry a giant inflatable penis.

To be fair to Emma, she wears the costume with pride, carrying the penis with her to the first club, where the rest of the girls are meeting us, and bumming us all with it along the way. I expect Jane and Co. to be absolutely horrified, but to my surprise they find the accessories a total scream, trying on Emma's garter and posing for photos with the inflatable penis between their legs. Once inside the club, they seem to have an even better time, immediately taking themselves off to the dance floor and whirling each other round, hooting with laughter. Relieved that the mums are enjoying themselves, us girls visibly relax and proceed to do what we do best . . . get absolutely shit-faced.

The first half of the night passes in the usual happy blur of shots, cocktails and humping chairs.

The second half gets a little . . . sticky.

Lagging a bit behind Emma and the rest of the group, Louise, my friend Anya and I try to follow them into another bar, which we are *definitely* on the guest list for. The problem is, we have walked through torrential rain to get here and I am at the point of drunkenness where I look as though my face has melted. Probably the least intoxicated of the three of us (though still absolutely poleaxed), Anya takes it upon herself to go and have a word with the bouncer, while I casually lean up against a nearby bin in what I hope is a coquettish position (it isn't), desperately trying to control my arm spasms and stop my eyes from wandering off in opposite directions.

The bouncer looks down at the guest list, surveys the state of the three of us and firmly shakes his head.

'ALLOW ME,' I demand, propelling myself from the bin and setting off purposefully towards him.

'Good evening, old bean!' I begin. (I don't know why, but whenever I'm extremely drunk and trying to act sober, I revert to what can only be described as stick-up-the-arse English. I once, after a night out, asked my parents whether they would like me to entertain them with my lute-playing. We don't own a lute.) 'My pals and I were hoping to enter your fine establishment in search of a few light ales. Or perhaps to shake a wicked hoof on the dance floor. But, BY GINGER! There seems to have been some sort of beastly mix-up with the guest list. Could you just be a ruddy good egg and let the three of us in?'

The bouncer looks bemused but also a little bit frightened. 'No, love.'

It is at that point that I lose it.

'What are you?' I demand. 'A MAN OR A MOUSE?!' (I don't know where I got this phrase from and hope to God that I will never feel the need to use it again.)

The evening then deteriorates further as we head to Chippy Lane – the street where the entire population of Cardiff goes at the end of a night for a bag of chips and a fight. I order myself a light bedtime snack of A KILO OF CHIPS, CHEESE AND GRAVY (just, don't) with some sort of pasty, which I like to think is cheese and onion but in all honesty is probably corned beef.

Armed with our fortifying and nutritious meals, Louise and I (having lost Anya somewhere around the kebab joint) somehow manage to find our way into a taxi. Here is where I get slightly confuddled. In London, I will always get an Uber home at the end of the night. Such is my love for the ease and convenience of Uber that I've even toyed with the idea of working for the company myself (before my friend reminded me what a horrific driver I am, and how I once followed my sat nav blindly and trustingly through a closed wooden gate).

The beauty of an Uber is that the fare is simply charged to your card, removing the need to pay in cash once you reach home. So as we pull up at our hotel, I cheerfully leap out of the taxi, slamming the door gaily behind me with a cry of 'THANK YOU, KIND SIR, AND GOODNIGHT!' before cavorting my way inside, leaving the taxi driver open-mouthed and outraged behind me.

We spend the rest of the night trying to order room service, but I am too pissed to realise that I need to use a telephone and am ashamed to say that I resort to crossly shouting at the menu, 'BURGER! BURGER! A DOUBLE CHEESEBURGER, PLEASE!' When a burger fails to materialise, I stagger downstairs in search of Emma.

She blasts through the glass revolving doors into the hotel foyer several minutes later, hiccuping and dragging along her veil, which has somehow fallen from her head and attached itself to her stiletto heel. She then proceeds to loudly order a Domino's while rolling deliriously around on the marble floor, flashing her garter. The hotel porter is so horrified by the whole affair that he promises to hand-deliver a pizza personally to her room as long as we all 'please leave the foyer now, ladies, please, FOR THE LOVE OF GOD'.

I'm just about to bundle her into the lift, both of us in extreme fits of giggles, when Natasha click-clacks her way across the foyer with a face like thunder, Emma's deflated penis folded and tucked neatly under her arm, like one might carry a copy of *The Times* while boarding the tube. Unlike the two of us, she appears to be completely sober – not a false eyelash out of place – and is not at all happy.

'I'll take her, Gabs,' she says, shoving me out of the way

and throwing me an accusatory stare, as if it is completely my fault that Emma is now pressing all the buttons in the elevator and singing 'I've Got A Lovely Bunch Of Coconuts'.

'Night, Bitchtits!' Emma hollers cheerfully, as Natasha closes the silver metal doors in my face.

'Night, Pegleg,' I mutter to myself. 'AND GOODNIGHT, WHORE-FACE!' I yell at the closed elevator.

A small cough behind me makes me jump.

'Will madam also be going up to her room?' asks the by now ashen-faced hotel porter.

'I'll take the stairs,' I hiccup, patting him on the bottom and cannoning off through what turns out to be a fire door.

11

Fat Camp

I have been on a diet for the past five and a half years. But if you were imagining me with the svelte, toned physique of an adolescent whippet, you'd be severely mistaken. Every fad diet I have undertaken has left me significantly fatter than when I started. They range from the sensible and well researched to the more ludicrous and extreme.

The Atkins diet is a mind-boggling phenomenon, where you are encouraged to stuff yourself with as much steak, sausage, pork chops and eggs as your fat little stomach can handle, while eschewing healthy things such as fruit and vegetables with a firm hand. Fools such as myself were very taken by the idea until learning that Dr Atkins himself had actually died of a heart attack.

Then came the baby food diet (where instead of breakfast, lunch and dinner, fourteen jars of puréed mush are consumed), the cabbage soup diet (initially the huge vats of watery cabbage you're consuming each day do appear to be doing the trick, until you end up so bloated and windy that you are unable to take public transport) and the werewolf diet (not, as I assumed, feasting by the light of the full moon, but in actual fact following a highly complicated eating plan according to the lunar calendar).

Needless to say, I would manage to follow each plan for two or three painful, stomach-growling, migraine-inducing days before running into the nearest corner shop like a junkie needing a fix and piling my basket with crisps, cookies and frozen pizzas, which I would then gorge on in my bedroom before falling into a disgusting gluttonous food coma. I fear the phrase 'I'll start tomorrow' will be engraved on my tombstone.

However, there comes a point in everyone's life when you think to yourself, enough is enough. Surprisingly, it didn't come for me in those three painful years at drama school, surrounded by stick-thin model-like girls. It didn't come when I broke that plastic chair in Year 7 maths class and everyone hollered 'WHO ATE ALL THE PIES?!' (I swear to this day that the chair leg fell down a hole in the floor.) It didn't come that time in Topshop when I got a summer dress stuck over my hips and had to physically RIP MYSELF OUT OF IT, then purchase the sorry item at the till.

No. For me, it comes the morning following Emma's hen do.

In an unpleasant half-drunk/half-hung-over state, my fellow bridesmaids and I stagger out of the hotel, blinking like moles in the harsh morning light, and pile into a rather green-looking Emma's car. In a horrible turn of events, this is the morning we are booked in to have our bridesmaid dresses fitted.

Taking my right shoe off and clutching it to my chest, ready to be used as a makeshift sick bag, I clamber in the back with Louise and brace myself for the journey.

Things are not helped, once again, by Jane coming with us.

It took poor Emma several attempts to pass her driving test, significantly hindered by lessons with her mother. Apparently on their first outing, as Emma tentatively did up her seat belt and moved into first gear, Jane announced, 'You know what you're driving, Emma? A DEATH MACHINE.'

Today is no different.

'There's a red light ahead, Emma!' warns Jane.

Emma visibly grinds her teeth. 'Yes, thank you, Mum.'

'It's still a red light, Emma . . . Red light, RED LIGHT!'

Only Natasha manages to look perfectly calm and composed, following in her own car with her colossal suitcase and Ceri as passengers, having found the time and wherewithal this morning to straighten her hair, spray herself with perfume and apply a perfect layer of make-up. Having slept in my own clownish, crusting slap, I am now in the process of chiselling it off with a face wipe and scraping my greasy, fag-scented hair into a bun.

Finally, with a final warning from Jane – 'It's a car, Emma, not a toy!' – we pull up green and shaking at the bridal boutique.

I've never actually set foot in a bridal shop before (I know this is rather stating the obvious, as I can't get a guy to even text me back, let alone marry me) and it completely lives up to my expectations, decked in soft white carpet, creamy suede furniture and row upon row of ivory and white dresses. Occasionally my eye falls upon the odd shocking red number with feathers sticking out, catering for the more daring of brides, who will no doubt have a themed wedding that all her guests will dread for months.

Instantly, a young and perfectly groomed woman bustles up to us, greeting Emma, Jane and (to my horror) Natasha with air kisses.

'So! These must be the lucky bridesmaids!' she says brightly, clapping her hands.

She manages to hide her slight grimace as she surveys the state of the three of us, clearly hoping that we won't touch anything or sit down on the furniture.

'Now then, Emma and Natasha have already been in and pre-selected some dresses for you to try.' (Confirmation of this intimate bestest-friend moment that I have clearly been excluded from punches me hard in the stomach.) 'So if you want to follow me through to the changing room, we'll let the fun commence!'

The dress Emma has picked out for us is actually rather lovely. Pale pink in colour, it is a Grecian wrap-around style that can be tied at the back in a variety of ways. Rather worrying, however, is the fact that it is 'one size fits all'.

'The beauty of this dress is the material,' the assistant informs us, handing us one each. 'It has a slight stretch to it, so no matter what your size, it will look fabulous. For you larger ladies,' she continues, rather rudely eyeing up myself and Louise, 'we can add a little vest top underneath to protect your, ahem, DIGNITY.'

As there is only one changing room available, we wait in line to try on the dresses and be scrutinised one by one. Natasha, of course, goes first, picking up her large designer handbag (complete with one of those irritating fluffy pompom key rings and a little photo of her and Emma on holiday) and swinging it on to her shoulder. It is unfortunate that in doing so, she manages to knock the head clean off a child mannequin, which proceeds to roll under the curtain of the changing room opposite. Panicked shrieks are then heard from within, some poor woman's magical dress fitting now forever tarnished with the memory of a child's face staring up at her from the floor.

'Sorry, oh God, so sorry,' flusters Natasha, hilariously making things worse by attempting to reach her hand under the curtain and retrieve the head herself.

I am reminded of a time several years ago when shopping in a department store with my mum. A very elderly (and clearly visually impaired) lady walked up to a child mannequin dressed in sports clothes and holding a football, and loudly cried in her thick Welsh accent, 'AWWW, BLESS, ARE YOU LOST, LOVE? WHERE'S YOUR MAM THEN?' before taking it by the hand and attempting to drag it across the floor to customer services.

Having composed herself after the mannequin incident (no doubt forbidden from being mentioned by anyone ever again), Natasha emerges from the changing room glowing and preening in her bridesmaid's dress. I mean, it looks great on her. Really great. Skimming over her size 8 body, hugging her pert boobs with no need for a vest top, complemented by her thick brown hair falling in waves on to her shoulders.

If there is one thing I am sure of at this moment in time, it is that this dress is not going to look like that on me.

Crammed into the tiny changing room, I manage to shoe-horn myself into the thing, while Emma and the assistant stand behind me trying to heave my double-D breasts up in order to tie the back. While Natasha's dress had adorable ruching on the front, my breasts have strained the material to its maximum capacity, giving it the sleek and shiny appearance of a large salmon.

Feeling my cheeks flaming in embarrassment, I walk out of the changing room to be assessed by the others.

'Very nice, Gabrielle,' says Jane unconvincingly. 'Give us a little twirl.'

Now feeling less like a salmon and more like a performing seal, I turn round, whereupon Jane gives a blood-curdling scream.

'AAAGHHH!! Gabrielle! What is that thing on your shoulder?'

Having absolutely no idea what she means, and worried that I might have inadvertently got a squashed chip or an old condom stuck to myself last night, I whip my head round to look in the mirror.

Ahh. Yes.

'It's a tattoo, Jane,' I explain patiently.

Two years ago, I decided to get a tattoo of a hummingbird on my left shoulder. I'd dithered about it for several years before thinking, 'FUCK IT!!' and choosing something large and wildly inappropriate that I would no doubt regret for the rest of my life. The tattoo has been a disaster for several reasons.

First, having been standing in front of a mirror at my appointment, I got the tattoo inked on to the wrong shoulder and am therefore permanently convinced that it's on the other side. Secondly, I fucking hate hummingbirds. Why oh why I chose the sodding thing in the first place I will never know. It would have made more sense to have something I actually love tattooed on to me, such as Tom Hardy or a doughnut.

'Does your mother know about this?' Jane asks beadily, as if I am a naughty toddler caught stuffing gummy bears into her knickers.

'Yes, yes, she does.' (I don't add that my parents spent five months convinced that my tattoo was a stick-on transfer before I finally plucked up the courage to tell them the truth.)

'Oh, what are we going to do?' frets Jane, wringing her hands in distress. 'It's awful. You can't go up the aisle looking like that.'

By this point I have had about enough and only just resist the overwhelming urge to rip off my dress and shove it up Jane's arse. But with gritted teeth I manage to keep it together for the remainder of the appointment, until I can finally escape on to the train back to London.

Perhaps there is something I can do about this situation. Although finding myself a date for the wedding is looking about as likely as seeing a flying pig, at least I can prevent myself from actually *looking* like that pig.

As soon as I get in, I whip out my laptop.

I find what I'm looking for pretty swiftly. Plugged as 'Europe's Leading Boot Camp', this place, based at a manor house in Suffolk, promises 'an intense week of army-style training and expert nutrition, leading to incredible results'. So, basically, fat camp in disguise.

I already know that I am severely unfit. This is brought sharply into focus every time I attempt to walk up the escalators in the tube station and have to give up halfway, nudging myself awkwardly into the queue of people on the right-hand side to let me in. I have had a gym membership for the past two years and have gone a shameful total of six times, meaning that each trip has theoretically cost me £96. It would have been cheaper and easier to get six sessions of liposuction. Nonetheless, I am determined to see this through.

This is it, I think excitedly to myself three weeks later, as I stuff trainers, towels and cystitis relief sachets into a large duffel bag. This is the start of a new me!

Gone are the days of rubbing Vaseline on my chafing inner thighs. Gone are the days of getting smacked in the face by my own breasts when running for the bus. Gone are the days of ordering myself a colossal Chinese takeaway, then feeling so embarrassed when the delivery man comes to the door that I shout, 'Food's here, guys!' into my empty flat.

It is difficult to describe my five days at fat camp, but here's the diary I keep of my ordeal.

DAY ONE

KILL ME NOW.

I cannot move my arms. Or face. I don't even know if I own legs any more. You know that scene in *1984* where Winston is sent to Room 101 to face his ultimate fear, rats? Mine right now would be an exercise bike.

I arrive in the afternoon on the train, dragging my three-stone suitcase along the platform, which is, quite frankly, a strenuous workout in itself. Having been told that a minibus will be coming to collect us all from the station at 2 p.m., I look around for the other fatties who have signed themselves up for the ordeal.

Expecting to see a group of panic-stricken individuals wolfing down their last bacon butties, I am somewhat perturbed to be greeted by a group of about fifteen Lycra-clad women, all looking completely fresh-faced, normal in size and excited at facing the challenge ahead.

'Afternoon, ladies!' comes a cry.

Turning round, I see a burly man hopping out of a minibus, dressed head to toe in army clothing. Phwoar. Ding-dong.

'My name's Staff Simmonds and I'll be your main point of contact this week.'

He looks meaningfully at my case as I attempt to pick it up and hurl it into the back of the bus with the others.

'Staying for a month, are you?' he asks, the bloody comedian.

'No, just the five days.'

It is at this point, annoyingly, that the make-up items I had secreted in the front pocket fall out and clatter across the pavement.

'Ha ha!' hollers Staff Simmonds. 'You won't be needing much of that, love. A few hours' training in the field and your face will be painted in mud!'

'Yes, well, I might want to freshen myself up for dinner,' I mutter, starting to get a little annoyed now and wishing this man would stop making such a spectacle of me.

This merely amuses Staff Simmonds further.

'DINNER?! Ha ha ha! Oh, you're in for a rude awakening this week, love. What's your name?'

'Gabby.'

'I'm going to call you Gobby.'

Excellent.

Pulling up at the house, we are then introduced to two more army men, who will be conducting our training for the next five days.

'Watch out for this one!' says Staff Simmonds jovially, prodding me in the back.

The house itself is beautiful – a huge honey-coloured manor with extensive grounds in which we will soon no doubt be screaming in pain.

One by one we pile into the dining room for the introductory talk.

'Welcome!' Staff Simmonds cries, looking around with a glint in his eye. 'You've signed up here because you want to make a significant change to your body in a short space of time. It ain't gonna be easy. If you've come expecting a relaxing spa break . . . '

His eye catches mine.

' . . . then you may as well leave now. During these next five days, Staff Lockwood, Staff Hocking and I are going to be putting you through your paces physically, mentally—'

'And spiritually!' chimes in a woman in the corner of the room who looks like a cross between Pat Butcher and a boiled egg.

'Er, yes,' says Staff Simmonds. 'Everyone, this is Cindy-Lou. She'll be doing a spot of life-coaching with you.'

'The future belongs to those who believe in the beauty of their dreams!' she twinkles at us.

Brilliant. She is basically Natasha Jones in thirty years' time.

'Your meals will be low in calories and high in fat-burning potential,' continues Staff Simmonds. 'You will most certainly feel hungry and often nauseous as your body adjusts, but this is completely normal. Now then. If anyone has secreted any forbidden items in their bags . . .'

He looks beadily round the room.

' . . . now is the time to hand them in. Just that one little slip can significantly impact your results this week.'

Everyone glances shiftily at one another, saying nothing. Then slowly, the woman three seats down from me draws out a half-empty packet of ginger biscuits from her coat pocket and places them on the table.

'Sorry, I ate them on the train,' she whispers.

She is followed by another woman, who guiltily unzips her backpack and takes out two tubes of Polo mints and an entire jar of coffee. Soon everyone is rooting around in their coat pockets and bags, making a pile of half-eaten sandwiches, chewing gum, squashed cereal bars and several mangy old sherbet lemons; items that had no doubt sat undisturbed for several years.

By now, I am in something of a cold sweat, feeling as

though everyone could sense the twenty Marlboro Lights and miniature bottle of gin tucked happily away in the inner zip pocket of my bag. Shakily I fish them out and place them on the table. Wanker.

'Good!' Staff Simmonds smiles with satisfaction. 'You'll now be shown to your rooms, and then I want you downstairs in half an hour ready for your first training session.'

Absolutely nothing could have prepared me for that first session.

'THAT'S IT, GOBBY, BEND THOSE ELBOWS!' cries Staff Lockwood, as I lie face down in the mud attempting to do a press-up.

'I can't,' I wheeze, the sticky, metallic and highly unusual taste of hard work forming at the back of my tongue. 'I truly can't.'

'No such word as can't!' he replies briskly, lying down opposite me so that we are practically nose to nose. 'You're going to keep up with my pace. And PRESS UP! TWO! THREE! FOUR!'

I don't know which mad fool came up with the theory that 'exercise makes you feel good'. Following our one-hour circuit-training session, I feel as though I am about to keel over and die.

Unfortunately, the hell isn't over, as we are forced to endure two hours of team games followed by a short hike before dinner. At the end of the hike I am relieved to see that the minibus has come to collect us.

'Oh, thank Jesus!' I cry, jumping on board and plonking

myself down into the nearest seat. Wondering where everyone else is, I look out of the window to see the army men absolutely keeled over with laughter.

Staff Simmonds sticks his head in.

'Bad news, Gobby . . . You're all pushing the bus home!'

He is not bloody joking.

Dinner is an extremely shocking and depressing affair. When Staff Simmonds mentioned 'fat-burning foods', I foolishly imagined we might be faced with a steaming plate of salmon, accompanied by a hearty portion of brown rice and vegetables, followed by something nutritious yet delicious for dessert, like chocolate-dipped banana pieces.

Instead, that first meal is comprised of a boiled egg, four runner beans and a thin slice of turkey. There is no dessert. Used to mammoth, Desperate Dan-sized portions, I can feel the first waves of nervous hysteria forming. Oh my God. I am going to be starved! STARVED!

It reminds me of when I used to go to sleepovers as a little girl. My friends' mothers would always give us much smaller portions than I was used to (due, I would imagine, to them having much smaller daughters), leaving me tear-ful and panicky at the thought of having to spend an entire night sleeping on the floor with a growling stomach. In the end it got so bad that my mother would send me off with an emergency picnic parcel of biscuits, grapes and a sandwich that I would quietly tuck into in the dead of night. Here, however, there is certainly no picnic parcel to be had.

I am sharing my bedroom with a French journalist named Esmée, who has been sent to the camp by a women's magazine in order to write an article about it.

'You mean to say you PAID for zis torture?!' she asks me incredulously after dinner, as we wearily change for bed.

In the night, something happens.

Perhaps it is the change of environment. Perhaps it's the lack of food. Perhaps it is the alien effects of exercise on my body. But I wake up at about 2 a.m. with what can only be described as an EXTREME FEVER. (I will later come to learn that this is called 'detoxing'.)

'Jesus wept!' I mutter to myself as I sit up in bed, boiling hot and pouring with sweat. Everything is agony. My head. My throat. Every limb in my sorry plump body pulsates and burns with pain. Shakily I swing my legs over the side of the bed and attempt to stand up.

'Aaagh!' I cry, as my knees buckle beneath me and I sink to the floor with a loud thump.

'What is zee matter?' mumbles Esmée sleepily.

Deciding that I should probably die quietly rather than disturb Esmée's sleep, I whisper that I am fine and set out on my grim and treacherous path to the en suite toilet.

As standing up is clearly out of the question and I'm too sore to crawl on my hands and knees, I resort to an ungainly slide across the carpeted floor, in the manner of a large, unfit slug, occasionally bashing into the wardrobe or a nearby chair in the inky darkness.

Finally I feel the cool tiles beneath my fingertips and

know that I have reached the bathroom. Grappling around, I tug on the light and with a supreme effort manage to heave myself on to the toilet and relieve myself of a very dubious bowel movement.

Then comes the real problem.

I cannot for the life of me get back up off the toilet. It is as if every joint in my body, once loose and carefree, has seized up and turned solid, like a . . . like a . . . (I am honestly trying to think of a better expression here) like an erect penis.

Resigning myself to the fact that I am staying here for the night, I lay my head against the edge of the cool sink, shut my eyes and will myself to sleep, only to be discovered a mere three hours later, door open and pyjama bottoms down round my ankles, by Esmée coming in to have a morning shower.

DAY TWO

The day starts with a 6 a.m. run, during which I throw up into a bush.

The army men seem to find my pain hilarious and refuse my piteous requests to be carried back to the house. In fairness, they are probably scared that they will put their backs out.

The run is followed by an hour's indoor boxing, an hour's circuit training and then my much-dreaded individual life-coaching session.

I cannot take the life-coaching seriously. It's about as

hocus-pocus as that time I went for a crystal-ball reading, where the fortune-teller turned out to be a complete charlatan who read my future from a plastic orb with 'Made in China' emblazoned on the side. And charged me £20 for the privilege.

I spend a ridiculous half an hour with Cindy-Lou, during which she intensely probes and interrogates me, desperate to find out some shred of dark, juicy information.

'So, Gabrielle,' she begins. 'Why is it that you've chosen to come here? Do you think it could possibly be some DEEP-ROOTED, DARK CHILDHOOD TRAUMA that makes it difficult for you to accept your body the way it is?'

'Er, no, Cindy-Lou, I think I've just eaten too many pies.'

'Ah! These pies . . . could they possibly symbolise the PIE OF TURMOIL COOKING IN THE OVEN OF YOUR SOUL, FILLED WITH THE SECRET AGONY OVER THE LIFE THAT YOU ARE NOT FULFILLING?'

In the end, I get so racked off with the whole thing that I blurt out, 'Well, frankly I'm a little constipated right now, Cindy-Lou.'

She leaps on this like a fly to shit (sorry).

'Constipation! Oh Gabrielle, I'm so glad that you have finally shared this. The faeces you are holding inside you are your body's way of clinging to past regrets and pain! Let them go! Let them go! Let the universe claim them back!'

In the end, I ask her to give me a bloody Senokot and leave me alone.

After this, it is actually quite a relief to be faced with an abs-toning class, an hour's stretching and another one and a half hours of team games, which involves crawling through the mud with a pretend rifle.

I have worryingly taken quite a shine to the rifle exercise. Probably because I am fantasising about shooting Cindy-Lou with it. Or myself.

DAY THREE

Can you build up muscle in your fingers? Because my fingers have definitely inflated overnight. To the point where they are starting to resemble giant clown hands.

It's absolutely sheeting down with rain here, but never mind, as the morning begins with three hours' outdoor 'fun and games'! WHOOPEE! This involves throwing ten-pound sandbags and chasing after them. Oh, what larks.

There is a distinct air of depression in the room at lunchtime, so the staff decide to cheer us up with the reward of a pudding. This causes great excitement, particularly from myself. I absolutely love pudding. In fact, I have been known to go into a restaurant and substitute my starter and main course for two puddings ... followed by pudding. What will it be? I wonder. Eton mess? A nice bowl of sticky toffee pudding, perhaps?

Oh, silly me! A quarter of an apple and a single almond. I kid you not.

The weather brightens up a bit after lunch, so we are taken out on a joyful twenty-three-mile cycle ride.

Staff Lockwood tells us that we will need padded cycling shorts, and if we don't have them then we will need to line the crotch of our leggings with a flannel or small towel. This leads to great hysteria. (We have basically all gone mad with lack of food.) My favourite woman on the course, Linda, comes downstairs with a gigantic beach towel stuffed into her trousers and a cry of 'SADDLE ME UP, LOCKWOOD, I'M READY FOR A LONG RIDE!'

The bike ride actually turns out to be a hoot. We are talking twelve unhinged women pumping up a hill with padded crotches, fluorescent bibs and special emergency bells. I'm sure I hear someone ask if we are out on day release.

Tempers, however, do run high halfway through, with one of our team jumping off and shouting, 'I'M GOING TO CHUCK THIS BIKE AT A FUCKING WALL!!!' Feeling like chucking the bike at a fucking wall myself, I bite my lip and soldier on, grimly thinking of my bridesmaid's dress and how much I don't want to explode out of it when going up the aisle.

The quietest of the three army men, Staff Hocking, appears to have taken a bit of a shine to me, to the point where he insists on cycling behind me the whole way and valiantly pushing me up the hills. I would normally be flattered by this rare show of male attention, but frankly I'm too exhausted to flirt and I'm starting to get a bit racked off with him. Leave me alone, you cretin.

Then, as we stop for a break, he goes off and PICKS ME A DAISY! Eurgh. Everybody thinks this is incredibly sweet. I am nearly sick in my mouth.

DAY FOUR

Oh God. Something rather disturbing happened last night. It was 10 p.m. and we were all walking to our bedrooms ready for the hell to restart at 5 a.m.

I say walking – what I really mean is waddling. I have basically become so stiff that the only way I can actually move is in a squatting position, like I'm riding a small invisible pig.

Suddenly Staff Hocking pops out from around the wall and pulls me aside.

'There's a pub down the road,' he says in a furtive whisper, his mad little eyes darting back and forth. 'They do an offer . . . two pints and a pie for ten pounds. Meet me there in half an hour.'

For a second I am too stunned to speak.

'Sorry,' I splutter. 'Sorry, Staff Hocking? You think you can tempt me out of fat camp . . . WITH A PIE? Christ, it's like some sordid Enid Blyton novel. What were you going to do next? Carve out a love letter for me in mashed potato? Lower me out of my bedroom window on a string of Cumberland sausages? Leave me a trail of chocolate bonbons leading to YOUR COCK?'

Feeling that I may have overreacted slightly (Staff Hocking stands red-faced and open-mouthed with shock), I do not wait for a reply, instead giving a 'hmph', tossing my head and trotting up the stairs to my bedroom like some porky and disgruntled racehorse.

DAY FIVE

The end. IT'S THE BEAUTIFUL END.

After the final morning of torture, we are lined up one by one to be weighed and measured like prize pigs.

Given that there are no mirrors at the camp, it is rather hard to estimate just how much weight we have all lost. But judging by my level of fatigue and starvation, I am imagining a hell of a bloody lot.

The first woman comes out of the weighing room joyfully announcing that she's lost eight pounds in five days. Not bad, not bad at all. She is followed by the next woman – ten pounds in five days! This is getting rather exciting.

By now I am starting to envisage having to buy a whole new wardrobe for myself. Golly, maybe I am even TOO thin?! Can people actually see me if I stand sideways? Perhaps I will have to go to another fat camp. To get FATTER!

Smiling dazedly, I skip into the room and on to the scales.

'Congratulations,' smiles Staff Simmonds. 'You've lost a pound!'

I'm not quite sure what expression I am pulling at this point, but from the slightly nervous way that Staff Simmonds looks at me, I can only imagine it is rather terrifying.

'I know it doesn't sound a lot,' he reassures me. 'But the great thing is, you are young, so will have built up loads of muscle!'

I finally manage to form words.

'A p ... a pound?' I stutter. 'A pound?!!! I COULD SHIT A POUND, LOVE!'

'But Gobby, the muscles ...'

'I don't want the muscles! Take them back! I wanted to come out of here looking waif-like and gaunt! Not ripped like fucking Popeye!'

I am still seething all the way back to London on the train, crossly stomping my way up to the on-board buffet car and buying myself a lard-smeared sandwich and several cans of pre-mixed gin and tonic.

Why the hell bother? I think grumpily to myself, throwing a large Kit Kat Chunky into the mix. May as well start as I mean to go on. Clearly I am one of those people carrying the fat and hairy gene. Like Bagpuss.

My self-destructive black mood carries on all the way back to my flat, as I stop off at the corner shop to buy myself a large packet of Haribo, a box of Mr Kipling's fondant fancies, some strawberry laces and a litre of Gordon's gin, like some alcoholic teddy bears' picnic.

Making sure that neither of my flatmates is in, I lay out

my feast on the living room floor and prepare to eat and drink myself into a gluttonous coma.

A couple of hours later, I am feeling distinctly more jolly.

Who the hell cares if I'm carrying a bit of Christmas cheer? I ask myself merrily, pouring neat gin straight down my throat and ignoring the fact that we are currently in the month of April. Boys love a bit of something to grab hold of.

I start flicking through the TV channels, hoping to find something trashy along the lines of *Sixty Stone and Loving It* or *It's Me or the Pie* to rally myself further.

It is then that my channel-hopping lands on the programme *Dinner Date*. For those who do not flick as far as channel 26 on their television sets, the premise of *Dinner Date* is simple: a man or woman goes for dinner at three different people's houses on consecutive nights, then subsequently chooses which one of them they would like to go on a proper date with in a restaurant.

I'll admit, it doesn't sound like the most scintillating viewing, but it does very nicely watched back-to-back with a hangover, as it requires very little emotional engagement or brainpower.

Tonight, however, in my booze-riddled state, it seems the wittiest and most brilliant thing I have ever watched. Suddenly I am hit by a brainwave. Why not apply myself? The fact that I am an extremely poor example of a woman, with loose morals, an alcohol problem and a flair for all things distasteful, does not bother me. Nor does the fact that I cannot cook to save my life, my few fruitless attempts resulting in me tearfully smacking the hob with a rolling pin and having to retire to my bed with smelling salts.

With another glug of gin and an excited cackle, I fire up my laptop and open the application form.

12

Dinner Fate

I don't expect to make it through.

Having sent off my application form, in which I blithely admit that the sum total of my cooking experience amounts to opening a tin of Chappie for our dogs, I put the whole thing to the back of my mind, filing it under 'drunken ideas that are hilarious at the time but won't seem so funny in the morning'. Such as that time I paid for a series of bell-ringing lessons.

I am staggered, therefore, to be rudely awakened by a phone call a mere ten hours later.

'Hello?' I croak, the harsh light searing through my thin curtains and stabbing me unforgivingly in the eyes.

'Hello, is that Gabrielle?' replies an extremely chirpy voice. Surely it is illegal to be that jolly at this hour of the morning.

'This is she.'

'Gabrielle, this is Jessica calling from the *Dinner Date* team!'

Bit by bit, the events of last night slowly piece themselves together in my mind, like some sadistic jigsaw.

Oh no. Oh no, oh no.

'We've just received your application form and think you sound great. Would you be around today for one of our team to pop over and do a quick interview? It would only take half an hour – just for us to see you on camera and have a quick look at your flat.'

I stagger into our open-plan kitchen/living room and suppress a small scream. It is a sea of crusty dishes, wine bottles and yoghurt cartons overflowing with fag ends. Surely this is a bad dream.

'Um, yes, that should be fine,' I reply, my brain moving at too sluggish a pace to formulate an excuse.

'Fantastic! I'll send our researcher Harry over at about midday.'

Shit.

And so, instead of crawling back into bed as I so badly

need to do, I find myself half an hour later on my hands and knees, muttering darkly as I scrub a disintegrated pizza box from the carpet.

Deciding that the dishes are too horrific to even contemplate (new forms of life seem to be growing at the bottom of the sink), I improvise by shoving the worst of them back into the cupboards and slamming the doors shut.

Once I have done my best in the kitchen – i.e., terribly – I turn my attention to my own frankly frightening appearance. Due to a very limited time frame, this involves shoving on a clean jumper, slapping on an industrial layer of foundation and blasting my hair with so much dry shampoo that I start to resemble Karl Lagerfeld.

The doorbell goes.

Having expected Harry to turn up with a full film crew in tow, with perhaps a director's chair and a catering van, I am somewhat surprised when he arrives alone, with a small camera bag slung across his shoulder.

'Come on in!' I smile, kicking a towering pile of unopened junk mail out of the way of the front door and ushering him into the living room 'Can I get you anything? Tea? Coffee? Gin and tonic?'

'Gin and tonic, please!' he replies, laughing.

'Excellent choice!' I beam, getting the bottle of Gordon's out of the cupboard and narrowly stopping a leaning tower of spaghetti-smeared plates from falling out with it. Cheerfully I slosh gin into two glasses and hunt round for the tonic bottle. 'I know it's here somewhere . . .'

Suddenly I notice Harry staring at the glasses in utter dismay.

'Sorry,' he apologises, looking down awkwardly. 'I thought we were joking. I don't normally drink at midday on a Thursday.'

Bugger.

'Ha ha, me neither! Only teasing!' I laugh rather too heartily, attempting to pour the gin back into the bottle, which causes it to cascade over my hands and on to the floor.

By now, denied my much-needed hair of the dog, and having spent the morning cleaning, tarting myself up and welcoming an INTRUDER into my home, I can feel myself entering a bit of a bad mood. I do not want to be doing this. I want to change back into my pyjamas, order a pizza and cry over *Lady and the Tramp*, wailing, 'NOBODY WILL EVER LOVE ME LIKE THAT DOG!'

Crossly I stamp my way over to the sofa, sitting down with a thump. I don't know what this interview entails, but I suspect that I am going to be a little cavalier with my answers.

'So, Gabrielle,' Harry begins somewhat apprehensively, positioning himself behind the camera. 'I'm going to fire a few questions at you. Try not to think too carefully about the answers, just say whatever comes into your head.'

'Okay!' I reply, thinking, boy oh boy are you going to regret saying that.

'Let's start with the type of guy you usually go for. Can you describe him in a couple of words?'

'MENTALLY UNSTABLE.'

'Right. Ha ha. Good. Um, let's move on to food. What's your favourite dish?'

'Fruit salad. But just the grapes. That have been fermented into wine.'

The interview carries on in a similar vein, Harry looking more and more pained and throwing furtive glances towards the front door.

'Okay . . . And the final question – how far would you be prepared to go for a first date?'

This one requires some thought.

'Ooh, gosh, let me see,' I dither. 'Um . . . a kiss and a cheeky finger, perhaps?'

Harry looks stunned. 'I meant travel-wise,' he whispers.

Assuming that I have completely blown it, I cheerfully show Harry the door, looking forward to pushing the whole debacle from my mind and never hearing from the team ever again.

It is with absolute horror, therefore, that I receive a further phone call three days later.

'Hellooo, Gabrielle!' shrieks Jessica. 'I've got some fabulous news for you. They absolutely loved your audition interview over at head office and have selected you for the show!'

The fag that I have been chugging away on falls out of my mouth.

'Now I know that you requested to be the one going on the dates, but instead we think you'd be fantastic as one of the five contestants!'

Oh, fuck it.

Jessica tells me that I need to think up a menu and submit it within a week. The 'lucky man' will then choose three out of the five menus, corresponding to the three women he will be going on dates with.

I numbly hang up the phone and stare at my reflection in the window.

Well. Could I go on the show? I mean, why not? Granted, I am a terrible cook. I am also a nightmare to date. And yes, there is a strong chance that I may disgrace myself in front of the entire nation. But I can't ignore the slight glimmer of hope at the back of my mind that this might actually lead to something. I've always picked my own men before, and where has that got me? To the shelf of eternal spinsterhood, that's where. Perhaps in the hands of experts, I could actually be matched to the man of my dreams.

Triumphantly I open my notebook and begin thinking up ideas for what I will cook.

Like a vision, it comes to me.

'I'M GOING TO DO A MEXICAN THEME!' I bellow down the phone to Robyn, having quickly explained the whole *Dinner Date* scenario and now beside myself with excitement. 'Good God, think of the possibilities! Sombreros, tequila, piñatas, comedy moustaches ... what's not to love?'

'But Gabs,' interjects Robyn. 'What food are you going to—'

'I could even perform an authentic Mexican dance! WITH MARACAS!'

Now if there is one thing I love, it's a sexual innuendo. I have the body of a young woman paired with the brain of a pervy uncle.

(One of my most shameful memories occurred a couple of years ago, when, having been fired from the wine club, I was interviewed for a part-time job as a receptionist.

'Right then,' the manager began. 'Everyone who works here is extremely busy, so you'll need to be on the ball. I can't be on top of you twenty-four/seven.'

'OY OY!' I replied, giving him a heavy wink. I immediately regretted it, my disgusting innuendo hanging like a bad smell in the room. Needless to say, I was not offered the job.)

Consequently, sitting at my laptop with a large glass of wine, I proceed to draw up the most sexually perverted menu known to humankind.

Fantastic! I think, reading over my handiwork with glee. If that doesn't grab my date's attention, nothing will.

Unfortunately, my menu is promptly sent back to me three days later, with an email explaining that it is 'too explicit to be broadcast before the watershed'.

I bring it along to the pub that evening for a second opinion.

'How on earth could you think that "stick your churro in my chocolate sauce" would be okay?' asks Katie, half-laughing, half absolutely disgusted.

'And "stuff my piñata"?' interjects Robyn.

'Yes, in hindsight the piñata line was a step too far. I'm definitely still having one, though.'

After a bit of editing with the help of the girls, in which my

menu goes from an 18 rating to more of a PG, all that is left
to do is sit back and wait to see if I am selected.

'Try not to worry,' a now rather weary Jessica reassures
me as I ring her up for the third time that week. 'The girls
that aren't selected are often invited back on the show at a
later date.'

I don't have TIME for a later date! I want to yell at her.
Don't you see, woman? I have precisely three months to meet
the love of my life, seduce him and then drag him kicking and
screaming to my best friend's wedding!

Finally, having spent the entire week obsessively checking
my phone every time I hear the slightest buzz (which often
turns out to be someone else's phone ringing, or the sound of
a builder drilling into some tarmac two miles away), I receive
the call I have been waiting for.

'It's good news, Gabrielle!' says Jessica. 'We had our guy in
this morning to film the menu-picking . . . and yours was one
of the three he chose!'

'FUCK, YES!' I scream, dancing in circles round the living
room. 'When will the date be?'

'We'll be coming to film at your flat two weeks from today.
I'll send you all the details through on an email. So all that's left
to do is get practising those dishes and prepare for your date!'

I do intend to practise my dishes. Really I do. It's just that
so many other things seem more important. Such as ordering
a life-sized cut-out Mexican man and taping him to the wall.

I take my theme very seriously. Determined that dinner
will end with us gaily smashing a piñata to smithereens,

releasing not sweets but miniature bottles of alcohol, I enlist the help of Katie.

'Could I have it on some sort of winch system?' I muse. I am completely carried away with the idea of myself crying, 'And now for dessert!!' at which point I'll turn a handle and the piñata will blast through the doors of the kitchen cupboard and weave its way into the living room. 'Perhaps we could screw hooks into the ceiling?'

Once Katie has pointed out that this is a stupid idea as a) my landlord would not be happy with me drilling holes in the ceiling and b) more importantly the miniature bottles would smash upon landing, we settle for tying the piñata to a piece of string from the door frame and stuffing it with gummy sweets.

'You can still serve alcohol at pudding, just don't put it in the piñata,' Katie says.

'Oh, believe you me, there SHALL be alcohol,' I reply. 'My plan is to get my date so utterly plastered that he can't remember the evening at all and in his embarrassment and confusion will pick me as the winner. I was thinking of doing mojitos to start, followed by wine at dinner and a shot of tequila between each course. It is the Mexican way.'

For my outfit, I originally intended to greet my guest wearing full authentic Chiapas dress. Having scoured the internet, however, I eventually go off the idea, conceding that they are expensive to buy, incredibly unflattering and that I will most likely catch the frilly sleeves on the hotplate and set myself alight.

In the end I settle for jeans, a T-shirt and a jaunty rainbow-coloured poncho that I will sling over my shoulders when my date arrives.

Despite the best of intentions, I end up doing no practice runs whatsoever.

The night before filming is spent sitting up in bed on the verge of a panic attack, rhythmically stuffing jelly babies up the piñata's arse. It has suddenly dawned on me that all the preparation that seemed so important at the time – arranging a string of paper lanterns, purchasing a second-hand ukulele and blowing up an inflatable cactus – mean bugger-all if I can't actually cook my date his dinner.

After eventually falling into a fitful sleep (having a nightmare that my arms turn into giant burritos), the dreaded day comes.

In contrast to my interview with Harry, Jessica and the cameraman arrive in a giant van filled with lights and equipment, which they proceed to stuff into my tiny flat.

'Do you mind if I pour myself a glass of wine?' I ask nervously, as a monstrously large camera is set up on a tripod, pointing into the kitchen.

'No, no, you go ahead!' smiles Jessica breezily, as she busies around rearranging the furniture.

'Okay, so we have two hours to film you cooking the food before your date arrives. That should be plenty of time,' says Ian, the cameraman. 'So if you just want to set up your things, we're ready to go.'

Having not thought to print out my recipes, I rather

precariously balance my laptop on the counter, open at a recipe for chicken fajitas. I then stand waiting for a further twenty minutes as Ian goes around shutting all the windows in the flat in order to drown out the noise of some street brawl outside, and drags over another huge light to further illuminate the already baking-hot kitchen.

Sweating profusely, I look down at my watch. Oh my God, it's 5.30 already. He's due to arrive at 7.30. I am never going to get this done in time.

'Okay,' says Ian, puffing his way back to the camera. 'When you're ready, Gabby. Just pretend I'm not here.'

Taking a deep breath, I look down at my laptop and begin following the first instruction.

'STOP!' bellows Ian as I reach to get a bowl out of the cupboard. 'That was too fast. I need to follow you with the camera, so if you could just bend down and get that bowl again please, but at half the speed.'

Trying not to hyperventilate, I shove the bowl back into the cupboard before bending to retrieve it again with comic slowness.

Bowl safely on the counter, I splash a bit of oil in the frying pan.

'STOP!' Ian yells again. 'You mustn't do things like that without warning me first. I'm going to have to completely change the camera angle and come to the left of you to film that.'

I quickly tip the oil into the sink and prepare to do it again. I glance at my watch: 5.45 p.m.

Having eventually, after much pausing and restarting, managed to chop up my vegetables, it is time for me to prepare the chicken. Shakily I wipe the sweat from my brow, not giving a damn any more how I look on screen.

'I'm just going to get the chicken out now,' I say, smiling at the camera, then sticking my head in the fridge for a few seconds' blessed relief.

With infinite slowness, in order to avoid another bollocking from Ian, I lay the chicken on the chopping board. As I stare at it, I feel my stomach do a worrying flip.

The thing is, having been a vegetarian for the majority of my life, I have had very little experience of handling raw meat. Any meat eaten in the past few years has been purchased drunkenly, pre-cooked in some form of fast-food outlet or kebab house. Never before have I been faced with raw chicken. And it REPULSES me.

'I'm going to be cutting the chicken into bite-sized chunks for the fajitas,' I say to the camera, ignoring the assortment of black spots appearing before my eyes. With sweating palms, I pick up the knife and press it into the pink flesh.

That's when it happens.

A surge of vomit like a tidal wave rises up my throat and into my mouth.

'BLEEERRRUGHHH!' I retch, shoving my hand in front of my mouth just in time. Then, dropping the knife with a clatter, I shove past Ian, knocking over a large light, which nearly crashes through the screen of the television, and make it to the bathroom, where I projectile-vomit up the wall and into the toilet.

I can't believe this is happening, I think to myself, head down the U-bend. I actually cannot believe this is happening.

Outside the door I can hear Jessica ringing anxiously through to her head office.

'Yes, she's throwing up as we speak,' I hear her say. 'Yes . . . yes . . . No, she's only managed to cut up a few peppers and get a chicken fillet out of the fridge.'

Eventually there is a gentle knock on the door.

'Gabrielle?' Jessica coos. 'Are you able to come out?'

Feeling distinctly green and shaky, I stand up and wobble my way to the door.

'We've decided to cancel your date,' Jessica informs me apologetically. 'He was very nice about it and hopes you get better soon. Luckily one of the other girls is going to take your place.'

'I'm so sorry,' I say.

And so, instead of whipping up a Mexican feast for the man of my dreams, I spend that evening being driven in the back of the filming van to the nearest walk-in clinic, where the doctor takes one look at me, rolls her eyes and swiftly sends me home again, having diagnosed me with being a drama queen with a minor case of gastroenteritis.

Watching my episode a couple of weeks later, I realise that they have chosen to cut me out of the show altogether (a worrying trend developing in my TV appearances). Instead, a voiceover cheerily informs the viewers that 'Unfortunately, Gabrielle was taken ill during filming, having contracted gastroenteritis.' I still have absolutely no idea what gastroenteritis actually is, so I quickly Google it. It turns out to be 'a condition causing vomiting and EXTREME DIARRHOEA'. So the entire nation has basically been informed that I had the shits.

You would think that after this utterly humiliating series of events I would decide to call it a day. Put my sorry reality TV career to rest.

Yet for some reason, perhaps because I provided them with such a roller coaster of high drama last time, I receive a call the following month inviting me back on the show. I have made it absolutely clear that under no circumstances will I ever cook again (not just on TV but in LIFE), so miraculously, they allow me to come back in the much-coveted role of the 'picker'. I need do nothing more than be wined and dined by three men and driven around in a taxi all week. PERFECT.

There is a lot more filming involved in the lead-up to the first date. Along with an interview to camera, I have to be shown doing my menu-picking, in which I will select the three unfortunate souls having to cook for me. I also need to be filmed engaging in a favourite hobby or activity.

Having put my foot down firmly over the frankly mortifying suggestion of standing on a stage and reciting a dramatic monologue to the camera (this, I fear, could be the final nail in the coffin of my acting career), we agree on me demonstrating my passion for horse riding. It is unfortunate, really, that I do not own a horse, and we are filming in central London.

The film crew get around this by persuading a local inner-city riding school to lend me one of their horses for the afternoon. Due to health and safety regulations I am not allowed to actually ride the horse. Instead, having waxed lyrical in my interview about what a keen and experienced horsewoman I am, I end up leading the animal round in a circle while wearing a hard hat, and then throwing a rug over it.

Next comes the menu-picking. For what amounts to just a few minutes on TV, the actual filming of this takes a laborious four hours.

'Sorry, Gabrielle!' the camerawoman calls. 'Could we just have a shot of you picking up menu number two, then staring at it as if you're really puzzled and having to think hard about who to choose? Perhaps you could drum your fingers on the table or scratch your head and go "hmmm"?'

I am a trained actor! I want to scream. I know how to bloody look puzzled!

The menus themselves are a little worrying. They range from a Beatles-themed meal comprising 'Sergeant Stuffed Peppers', 'All You Need Is Pie' and 'John Lemon in Strawberry Fields Lemon Meringue Pie' to what is clearly a menu written by a cockney student, including 'A Cheeky Spag Bol' and ''Ello Treacle Tart'. There is a very humiliating moment when I misread 'White Chocolate Lattice' as a 'White Chocolate Lettuce', but somehow I manage to bumble my way through, selecting three of the least offensive-sounding menus.

Finally, with the pre-filming done, it's the morning before my first actual date.

As per usual, I find myself completely unprepared.

This includes hair at the back of my head that I have

neglected to comb, so that it manages to actually form a dreadlock (which I resort to cutting with a pair of kitchen scissors, leaving a small, chilly bald patch), a black finger-nail that I drunkenly trapped in a toilet door the previous weekend, ten pounds of extra weight gained (morphing into three extra chins, like Desperate Dan) and not a single outfit to wear.

'HELP ME!' I sob down the phone to Robyn. 'I have noth-ing to wear and I'm morbidly obese. Every dress I try on makes me look like Dame Edna.'

'What you need,' advised Robyn, 'is those sucky-in pant things. You know, the big elasticated granny ones. They knock inches off.'

Transfixed by a vision of my four-chinned head balancing on the svelte body of Kate Moss, I buy myself a very skimpy tight playsuit from Topshop before heading to M&S.

Ignoring the gangs of pretty young girls pondering over lacy pants with their boyfriends, I doggedly follow the stream of elderly women to the 'corrective underwear' section, where I survey the garments in horror. God, they are terri-fying. Like some medieval method of torture. Also what size does one go for? The size one actually is or the size one would ideally like to become after putting them on?

Eventually I settle on a sturdy-looking Lycra number, complete with little elasticated legs that extend over the thighs (a bit like an adult babygro without the arms), and head home.

As soon as I try my outfit on, however, it becomes clear

that there is a hideous problem. The legs of the giant pants extend BEYOND THE LEGS OF THE PLAYSUIT.

'No . . . oh no, oh no, oh no,' I wail, grabbing a pair of scissors from the kitchen drawer and proceeding to hack away at the pants.

This, it transpires, is a grave error.

Once cut, both knicker legs proceed to lose all their elasticity, rolling upwards and forming two small sausage rings at the tops of my thighs.

Realising that I only have an hour until my pre-booked taxi arrives, I give up on the playsuit, hurling it angrily into the corner along with the scissors and the mad pants. Instead, thinking TO HELL WITH IT! I sling on a comfy top and loose-fitting trousers and pour myself a glass of wine.

I am halfway through my taxi journey, en route to my first date's house, when my mobile goes off.

'Hi, Gabrielle,' says a rather stressed-sounding Jessica. 'I'm afraid there's been a bit of a hiccup. Our camera broke this afternoon and it's taken us a while to get it going again, so your date has only just started cooking his food. Would you mind waiting in a bar nearby and we'll send another taxi to collect you when we're ready?'

'No problem!' I reply cheerfully, instructing the taxi to drop me off at a bar up ahead. 'I'll just order myself a drink and wait for you to call.'

I should have known that this was never going to end well. Wandering up to the somewhat deserted bar, I order myself a gin and tonic, then sit quietly in the corner.

Date delayed!! I send in a group message to my friends. *Sat in bar, on own, waiting!*

Oh DEAR GOD, comes back Emma's immediate reply. *You are going to get hammered ha ha ha.*

DON'T GET TOO DRUNK!! says Robyn.

LOL. What number glass of wine are you on? Or should I say bottle? asks Katie.

Oh ye of little faith.

It is then that the barman catches sight of me.

'Been stood up, have you, love?' he asks, winking.

'No ... well, not exactly,' I explain, bridling slightly. 'I'm about to go on the programme *Dinner Date* and there's been a delay.'

That does it.

'Oh my God!' cries the barman in excitement, turning round to holler into the kitchen. 'Janine! JANINE!!! This girl is about to go on *Dinner Date!*'

Next thing I know, three Jägerbombs have been placed in front of me, as the barman, who introduces himself as Greg, and Janine (an avid *Dinner Date* fan) cluster round excitedly.

Half an hour later, I am absolutely plastered.

'I dunno where the blurry film crew are blurry gone,' I slur as Greg fills up my glass again. 'But I am beyond blurry caring.'

I pause dramatically, raising my drink.

'If they cannot handle me drunk ... then they DO NOT DESERVE ME SOBER!' I declare, feeling that I may have got the saying mixed up somewhere along the way.

I am just considering packing the whole thing in and inviting Greg back to mine for a game of Twister and more gin when my phone goes off.

'Hi, Gabrielle!' pants Jessica. 'I'm so so sorry for such a long delay. I hope you haven't been too bored?'

'Not in the slightest,' I slur.

'Great. Well tell me where you are and I'll hop in my car and come and pick you up.'

I reluctantly bid goodbye to Greg and his team, promising to let them know when the episode airs, then cannon out of the door and on to the street, where Jessica is already waiting.

'Christ, are you all right?' she asks, as I sway precariously on the pavement.

'Absolutely dandy,' I reply, trying hard to focus on one of her six revolving heads.

It is only a short drive to my date's house, where everything is set up to film my arrival. Suddenly finding the whole situation hilariously ludicrous, I knock on the door as the camera starts rolling, and find myself face to face with a tall, thin man about my own age, dressed in tight black jeans and a black polo-neck sweater.

'HELLO!!' I beam, clutching the door frame for support.

Well. He does not look pleased to see me. Quite the opposite, in fact. For a second I wonder whether I have accidentally knocked on the wrong door.

Introducing himself as Pete, he eyes me suspiciously before allowing me inside, looking as though he would rather welcome anyone in – a tramp, a mass murderer, the entire cast of *Cats* – ANYONE other than me.

Sullenly he leads me into his living room, which has apparently been set up with what can only be described as garden furniture – green plastic table and chairs, and what looks like a curtain slung across in place of a tablecloth.

'Lovely!' I enthuse.

We sit down awkwardly on the sofa.

Pete does not take my coat or offer me anything to drink. Luckily I have an emergency bottle of white wine in my handbag, and I pour us two glasses.

'Cheers! Here's to the date!' I beam at him. He stares stonily back.

'You guys talk amongst yourselves for a minute,' Jessica interjects. 'We just need to set the camera up in the kitchen.' She leaves us in deafening silence.

'So,' I continue brightly. 'How has the cooking gone to—'

'I wanted to cancel this, you know,' he suddenly interjects, looking furious. 'I tried to call it off at the last minute but they wouldn't let me. They said it was too late.'

Well, clearly this evening is going to be an absolute barrel of laughs.

Thankfully, we are separated to film our first impressions to the camera.

'Well, he's not my usual type, but I'm really looking forward to getting to know him,' I enthuse, deciding to give him the benefit of the doubt.

Poor Pete, I muse, as I'm sent upstairs to wait. Perhaps he's just shy and not used to female company. The poor man is clearly so dazzled by my sparkling wit and good looks that he can barely speak!

Clutching my glass, I creep out to listen at the top of the stairs.

'WELL, IT'S SAFE TO SAY THAT I'M NOT ATTRACTED TO HER IN THE SLIGHTEST,' I hear him loudly declare.

I splutter quietly into my wine.

'She's very loud. And there's absolutely no spark there,' he concludes.

No spark? No spark?! YOU'RE TELLING ME, LOVE! Christ, getting conversation out of you was like getting blood out of a fucking turnip!

'And I didn't like to say anything,' I'm sure I hear him add, 'but she's clearly been drinking before she arrived. She's absolutely plastered.'

That does it.

'RIGHT! I'M READY FOR MY STARTER!' I cry, stamping crossly down the stairs and planting myself heavily on a garden chair, nearly falling through it.

The evening goes steadily from bad to worse.

Clearly desperate to get rid of me, Pete sulkily brings out each dish (which even by my culinary standards are absolutely appalling), takes a couple of bites and then puts his knife and fork down, announcing that he is finished.

This leaves me hastily wolfing down mouthfuls of undercooked chicken pie before placing my own knife and fork together with a clatter, which Pete also finds reason to complain about.

'Actually,' he snivels, 'you should always place your fork face down on the plate.'

Although this is quite clearly utter nonsense, I do what I'm told, worried that disobeying will send him completely over the edge.

In between courses, I neck back as much wine as I can in retaliation. Plastered? I'LL SHOW YOU PLASTERED, LOVE.

Finally it is time for dessert. I'm not quite sure what has gone wrong in the cooking process, but Pete's raspberry coulis appears to have taken on an extremely runny, watery consistency.

'Ooh, it looks like Ribena!' I jokingly remark, trying to lighten the mood.

Now, this show is supposed to be a laid-back, warm bubble bath of a programme. It's aired before the watershed. The height of drama is usually someone not taking their quiche out of the oven in time.

The camera team are astounded, therefore, by what follows next.

'So, now that the meal is over, I would like to say a few things,' announces Pete, placing his spoon and fork together (face down).

I smile encouragingly, thinking he is going to apologise for his bad temper and perhaps whip out a bottle of vodka.

'I feel that you've been fake-laughing the entire evening,' he says, 'and fake-smiling. In fact, you've been mocking me all night.'

I stare, flabbergasted.

'I haven't, honestly,' I stammer, completely thrown. 'I just laugh all the time.' I refrain from adding, ACTUALLY IT HAS BEEN NERVOUS LAUGHTER, YOU STRANGE AND INSANE LUNATIC. TONIGHT HAS BEEN DREADFUL.

Instead, we hastily wrap up the evening, hugging one another awkwardly goodbye before I am deposited out on to the street.

Now then, I am not usually a crier. I will literally do anything to prevent any emotions other than 'jolliness' and 'gaiety' from airing in public. But the combination of fresh air, tiredness and about four litres of different types of alcohol suddenly gets to me.

'THAT WAS THE WORST DATE IN THE HISTORY OF THE WORLD!' I sob, camera still rolling. 'He was r-really mean and his food was h-horrible. I'm t-tired, my chins are weighing me down and I . . . I JUST WANT TO ORDER A DOMINO'S AND GO HOME!'

I awake the next morning hugging the toilet bowl in my flat.

Oh God. The bar. The argument. The tears. How on earth did things get so bloody out of hand?!

I would rather do anything tonight, I think wearily. Colonic irrigation, church camp, waxing Natasha's back . . . ANYTHING other than go on another date.

And yet, at 7 p.m., I find myself standing outside my flat clutching two bottles of wine (I am taking no chances this time), ready to hop in the taxi to date number two.

Thankfully there are no camera mishaps this time and I arrive at the flat at the prescribed time of 7.30 p.m. Cameras once again rolling, I knock on the door, preparing myself for another angry minger to be standing on the other side.

It opens.

SHIT A BRICK! I almost cry out.

This guy is hot. A real hunk. As opposed to last night's date, who was dressed like a mime artist, this one is wearing jeans and an open-necked shirt, perfectly offsetting his sandy blond hair and wickedly blue eyes.

'My name's Daniel,' he smiles.

'Mmmnssgabrielle,' I slur lustily, hastily stepping inside before my loins catch alight.

Noticing that this man is having a drastically different effect on me, the camera team usher me off to film my first impressions in another room.

'Well, ding-dong!' I whistle, winking into the camera like some sexually aroused pensioner. 'He's a bit of a dreamboat, isn't he? MOTHER MAY I!'

I am then led, red-faced and panting, into the living room, where Daniel is waiting for me with a glass of wine. My jaw drops.

You know how in horror films a character will flick on the light and see things written in blood all over the walls? Well, this was one of those hideous, dawning moments. Except in Daniel's living room it wasn't writing ... it was Lego men. Wall-to-wall Lego men.

'Gosh!' I exclaim, looking around and feeling the eyes of

three thousand tiny plastic characters staring back at me. 'Do you collect these?'

'Yes,' replies Daniel. 'I actually have an Instagram account. I like to take the figures out and about, photographing them.'

'So you take them on ... day trips?'

'Yeah, I guess so.'

Excellent.

Despite this slight hiccup, however, the date goes from strength to strength. In fact, the beauty of Daniel is that, unlike Pete, he proceeds to get equally as sloshed as I do.

'Would you like to see my didgeridoo?' he suddenly asks during the main course.

'Sorry?' I stammer, choking on my salmon. 'Well, normally, yes, of course. But what with the cameras rolling ... '

'My instrument!' he replies, bounding up and getting an actual didgeridoo off the shelf.

'Oh!' I sigh in relief, taking a swig of wine and watching as he performs what sounds like a series of loud farts. 'That is most impressive.'

'Time for another bottle!' cries Daniel, stumbling through to the kitchen, followed by the sound of crashing pans and gushing water.

It is at this point that I realise I have completely forgotten my date's name.

'Shit, what is it?' I whisper to the camera, snorting with laughter. 'Draco? Derek? Domino? COME ON, DESMOND, BRING THAT WINE THROUGH!'

Clearly thrilled that we have hit it off, the camerawoman then asks if I will be giving him a goodnight kiss.

'A kiss? I'll be doing more than that, love,' I cackle. 'Pants down, Donald!'

Having crashed out of the front door at about 10 p.m., assuring Daniel that I will, without a shadow of a doubt, be picking him as the winner, I stumble into a taxi and am driven home.

If I wasn't feeling top-hole for my second date, by the evening of my third I am feeling very ill indeed. A case of the wooden mouth, as my grandmother would say. Hung-over, bloated and tired, I heave myself into the taxi to be taken to my third and final date's house.

If there's one thing I have taken away from this experience, I think crossly as the taxi lurches over a speed bump, causing me to do a little sicky burp in my mouth, it's that I will never complain about not having anyone to date ever again. Gone is the desire to truss myself up like some prize Christmas turkey and make awkward small talk all evening. I want to be sitting in my pyjamas watching *The Apprentice* and preparing for a life of solitude.

Wearily I get out at my final date's house just as Jessica runs up to meet me.

'Hey, Gabrielle,' she exclaims. 'We're pretty much ready for you.' She lowers her voice. 'Just to warn you,' she whispers, signalling that the microphones are switched on, 'your date is very nervous. So just be your usual bubbly, witty self.'

Oh brilliant, I think darkly. This is just what I need. I feel about as witty as a pool of sick.

Plastering what I hope is a calming and beatific smile on my face (though it probably looks more mentally deranged than anything), I knock gently on the door.

It opens slowly.

The man standing in front of me does indeed look as though he is about to shit his pants.

'Hello,' he says, holding out a sweaty palm for me to shake. 'My name's Raymond.'

Right. This is going to need two large doses of wine, swiftly followed by several shots, I think sagely, diagnosing the situation like some alcoholic doctor. I reach into my bag for my emergency wine bottle.

Amazingly, though, the emergency bottle is not needed. Perhaps having been tipped off by the film crew that the only way to placate me is to drown me in booze, Raymond has laid on enough alcohol to fill an Olympic-size swimming pool.

He isn't even repulsed when I lap him by three glasses of Prosecco, instead handing me the bottle to finish.

'This is smashing.' I grin at the camera, merrily sloshing white wine into my glass. 'I'm not sure I fancy him, but he's made such an effort. There are flowers on all the tables. And candles in the loo. And he's promised me that I can take the remaining wine home with me for the taxi ride!'

Raymond is indeed the perfect gentleman – filling up my glass as soon as it's empty (no easy task) and pretending not to mind when I barely touch any of his food. Those who know me will be rather shocked by this, as I rarely leave anything on my plate. In fact, I have been known to lick clean both my plate and that of the person next to me (providing I know them). But I will tell you now, if there's one thing guaranteed to put you off your food, it is being filmed while eating it, with a gigantic camera about an inch from your face. Suddenly every forkful makes you feel like Jabba the Hutt.

By the end of the night I am in such roaring spirits that I even agree to send a photo of us both to Raymond's mother.

'HELLO, MRS RAYMOND!' I beam drunkenly down the lens, as if this is not a photo but a Skype conversation. 'I would just like to congratulate you on raising such a lovely, LOVELY young man. So kind and considerate, with such excellent taste in wine and a delicate hand at flower arranging.'

Hiccuping and singing down the drive like a loon on her way back to the asylum, I hug Raymond goodbye and get into my taxi home. On fine form himself, the taxi driver then joins me in a rousing rendition of 'Total Eclipse Of The Heart' on the radio, and I fill him in on the juicy details of my dates.

'The first one had such a gigantic stick up his arse that I'm surprised it didn't poke out the top of his head like a Teletubbies aerial,' I cackle.

It is only when I get home that I discover five missed calls on my mobile and a hysterical voicemail from Jessica informing me that I have spent the entire journey with my microphone still attached.

It is then time for me to select a winner out of the three men.

I am sorely tempted to pick date number one – 'Congratulations – you've won ANOTHER EVENING WITH ME!' – as the ultimate punishment, but decide that it would be just too cruel. Despite having sworn to choose date number two, I find myself so drunk and confused from the previous night that I pick Raymond instead, purely because he is the only one I can remember clearly (my own original plan backfiring on me).

Our winning date is filmed in the basement of an extremely busy restaurant – the barren emptiness downstairs a stark contrast to the hustle and bustle above. It soon becomes clear that neither Raymond or I really fancy one another. Instead we tuck into our meal as best we can at our table for three – me, Raymond and the four-stone camera.

Conversation is more than a little stilted.

'So whereabouts did you grow up?' asks Raymond.

'Well, I was born in Wales and—'

'SORRY, RAYMOND,' interrupts the camerawoman. 'We didn't quite catch that. Would you mind repeating it again?'

'Um, sure,' he replies, severely flustered.

'So where did you, um, grow up?' he asks again, the whole conversation now delivered in the stilted manner of a school play.

Finally the camera team pulls me outside to deliver my parting diagnosis on the evening.

'Well, we definitely won't be seeing each other again but it's been a great evening,' I conclude.

'Hmmm, sorry, Gabrielle, could you reword that ever so slightly?' asks the camerawoman. 'Maybe more along the lines of "it's been a steamy little evening and romance is in the air"?'

'But it isn't.'

'Yes, but just to keep our viewers happy.'

The episode airs several weeks later. I know it's going to be bad when in the preview the voiceover says, 'And what NOT to do on a first date . . .' before showing me drunkenly arguing with Date No. 1 about his raspberry coulis before being ejected from his house.

Worse still is the ending. Having exchanged numbers with Raymond since the show but nothing more, I am absolutely astonished when the viewers are told, 'Gabrielle and Raymond are arranging their next date!'

Great, I think, sulkily lighting a fag while my friends howl with laughter in the background. Clearly my sorry love life is too depressing even for daytime viewing.

13

Chastity Knickers

The problem with going on a reality dating programme is that everyone automatically assumes you're up for it. A bit of a minx. A hair-fluffing, lip-puckered JEZEBEL.

Having spent the past year desperate for the merest whiff

of male attention, I suddenly find it coming in droves. But, alas, it is the wrong sort of male attention.

No sooner does my sordid little episode air than I begin receiving emails, Facebook messages and tweets from various men offering their services – valiantly volunteering to take me off the shelf for the night, give me a bit of a dusting and then presumably put me back where they found me.

Some of them are quite frankly farcical. I start to receive daily emails from a man named Colin, a self-confessed *Dinner Date* fanatic, who starts each of his excruciatingly boring ten-page missives not only as if we are life-long friends, but also mid-conversation.

They go along the lines of: *Hello, Gabrielle! Terrible weather, isn't it? My kettle has blown, so I'm off to my local Morrisons to get a new one. Do you have a kettle? May pick up some bread while I'm there and probably some Müller yoghurts. Do you like Müller yoghurts? They've got an offer on the Fruit Corner ones, although not the Crunch Corner ones, which is a shame as they're my favourite, although probably not so great for my teeth since I had a new filling done. Do you have any fillings? Probably not, your teeth looked really good on the programme. What toothpaste do you use?* Et cetera, et cetera.

I also receive a healthy amount of Twitter trolling. One girl takes a particular dislike to me and angrily tweets throughout the show, pointing out that the Welsh for 'microwave' is in actual fact *meicrodon* (not *popty ping* as I drunkenly taught my date), accusing me of putting on my 'posh accent' and, as a final hurrah, tweeting, *What's up with her hair? #lumpy.*

Another troll, upon seeing the delectable salmon dish cooked for me by date number three, tweets, *A fishy feast? A bit like Gabrielle's fishy vagina then,* followed by a selection of aquatic-themed emojis.

Although a little shocking, they don't offend me and make for hilarious reading at the pub. I reason with myself that the only thing sadder than actually going on *Dinner Date* is watching it and then tracking down the participants afterwards.

However, there is one message that does truly shock me. It comes from a boy named Jake, who differs from all the others for two reasons: a) We actually know one another, him having been in the year above me at drama school, and b) I FANCY THE BLOODY PANTS OFF HIM.

Let me tell you now, this boy is an absolute humdinger. Tall, smouldering, with a mess of dark hair and a strong pair of thighs, he is, and always has been, completely out of my league. So much so that we went two years together at drama school without so much as exchanging a single word. I wisely learned to lust from afar, surreptitiously ogling him through my gin glass at the pub, while he flirted and hung out with the thinner and cooler girls.

We are not even friends on Facebook, so his message comes completely out of the blue.

Hey Gabby . . . Just watching you on Dinner Date! ;)

My heart jumps into my mouth.

Oh no! How embarrassing. I would pay them to stop repeating it!! I reply, simultaneously thinking, THANK YOU, REALITY TV GODS! I WILL LITERALLY PAY YOU TO

KEEP REPEATING THIS EPISODE TILL THE END OF MY DAYS!

This leads to a flirty little exchange of messages, me assuring Jake that I am, amazingly, still single and him gently taking the piss out of me for going on the show.

There is, admittedly, a humongous elephant in the room, which I choose to ignore. Why, having spent two years under the same roof as me and not having shown the slightest shred of interest, is Jake suddenly attracted to me now? Not wanting to ruin the magical moment, I shrug this thought off, convincing myself that he must have been won over by my on-screen wit and, um, scintillating conversation.

Finally the moment I have been waiting for comes.

Don't suppose you fancy grabbing a coffee or a drink soon? he asks.

YEEES!

I shut my eyes and try to compose myself.

A drink sounds good, I reply coolly, completely ignoring the frankly ludicrous suggestion of coffee. I've never understood people who choose to have a non-alcoholic first date. Surely the whole idea is to calm your nerves with booze, both get a bit whoopsie and then do things that you'll cringe over for years to come. You can also tell a lot about a man's personality from the booze he orders on a date. Beer? Fine. Wine? Fine. Bacardi Breezer? Run for your life.

We arrange to meet up the following Friday, with me thinking that this will give me adequate time to lose half a stone, get my roots done and wax my centaur legs. I really, really like this guy and am determined not to fuck it up.

Gleefully I imagine the look on Natasha's face were I to march into the wedding in just two weeks' time with Jake on my arm. Plus, my parents would be so happy.

Friday finally comes and I am about to go through the roof with nerves. Will he still fancy me in the flesh? Will we have enough things to talk about? Having given Jake a thorough Facebook stalk, I know him to be doing extremely well in the acting industry, so make a mental note to steer conversation towards his acting achievements and, please God, away from my own.

We have already arranged to meet in one of the lovely bars on the South Bank, so I am surprised to receive a further message from Jake on Friday morning.

Good news, he says. *I've got no work this weekend so we can be proper nightowls!!!* ;)

Great! See you there at 7 p.m., I type back, somewhat bamboozled by the night-owl analogy. I am pretty sure all the bars on the South Bank shut at midnight. Surely he isn't suggesting that we go on . . . clubbing?!

You still live near Chiswick, right? I can meet you there if you like? he suggests. *Haven't been back in ages.*

This is where alarm bells about Jake's intentions for the evening should have started to ring. Clearly he is not really dying to come back to the most boring area of London, in which he has already spent three years. Clearly he is not some sort of owl enthusiast. However, being insanely in denial and completely carried away by the idea of him, I merely think to myself, awww, how sweet! He's offering to come all the way across town to save me the journey! HE MUST REALLY LIKE ME!

Nevertheless, I insist on meeting at the station on the South Bank, partly to save poor old Jake the journey and partly due to the new wine bar there that I am gagging to try out.

Having spent three hours painstakingly applying my make-up and taking on and off about forty different outfits, I am finally ready and hop on the tube. I am three stops away when I realise that I really need a nervous poo. I can't disappear to the toilet as soon as we get to the bar, it will be too awkward. I'm going to have to find somewhere before I meet him.

I whip out my phone and send a quick message.

Hey Jake, running a little late! Can we meet at the bar instead, in about 20mins?

Jumping off the tube at Embankment and barging my way through the barriers, I set off at a purposeful waddle in the direction of a nearby Starbucks.

'Hey, Gabby!' comes a man's voice.

BALLS. Too late.

'Oh, there you are,' I gabble nervously as Jake draws me in for a hug, 'I, um, got here a little quicker than I thought so decided to get a coffee, but now that you're here, OFF TO THE WINE BAR WE GO!'

'It's good to see you,' he laughs.

I finally allow myself to make eye contact. BLISS ON A

STICK. He is even more of a flutter bum than I remember. What the hell is he doing here with me?

We arrive at the bar and I finally make it to the loo, under the pretence of having to powder my nose (aka taking a shit). When I arrive back, I'm thrilled to see that Jake has already been up to the bar and ordered us two large glasses of Merlot. Massive Brownie points immediately.

'Cheers!' I say, taking a big gulp.

EEURGH. Having cleaned my teeth about five times before I left, the wine has mixed with the toothpaste in my mouth to form a disgustingly acidic taste.

I look across at Jake and am surprised to see that he is also grimacing.

'I've just cleaned my teeth,' we both say together.

OH MY GOD.

After that, the date goes from strength to strength. He is really funny. And amazingly, he seems to find me quite amusing, too. Tongue loosened by my second glass of wine, I decide to move the conversation on to my entrepreneurial pursuits.

'I've come up with an idea for *Dragons' Den*,' I declare confidently.

Jake grins at me. 'Go on then.'

'You have to swear to me you won't steal it.'

'I won't steal it.'

'You'll want to steal it, it's very good.'

'I promise I won't steal—'

'THE CHILLOW!'

Pause.

'What?'

'The Chillow. It's a pillow that stays cold on both sides.'

'What about if you like a hot pillow?' Jake asks, not looking quite as bowled over by my idea as I had expected.

'Who likes a hot pillow?'

'I do. In the winter months.'

'Well then, especially for freaks of nature such as yourself, I would create a further line of specially heated pillows. Called ... called ...'

'Yes?'

'The Grillow.'

And that is the moment when Jake gives a big belly laugh and draws me in for a snog.

I am very grateful that my acne has cleared up in recent years, as he has a lovely way of cupping my face as he kisses me and stroking my cheek with his finger. In fact, it is hands down the most tender and romantic first kiss I have ever had in my life.

'Shall we move on to another bar?' he says, as I sit there reeling.

And we walk along the South Bank together, all bustling restaurants and twinkly lights, HOLDING HANDS.

I can say with absolute certainty that I haven't held hands with a boy since I was about seven years old. Even past boyfriends never held my hand, instead preferring to just sling an arm round my shoulder. The only slight difficulty with the hand-holding is that Jake and I are clearly of equal height, therefore in my heels I have become a couple of inches taller than him. Not wanting to ruin the moment, I find myself ambling along at a light trot, knees bent, feeling distinctly like Mr Tumnus.

Despite this, a smile creeps its way across my face. This is truly unbelievable. I am on a proper first date with a boy I really like, who has kissed me nicely and held my hand. A far cry from my usual 'dates', where both parties get absolutely plastered, throw up in a bush, have sex and then never speak again. This is how it should be done. I hardly dare let myself believe it, but there is a slight chance that this could lead to a real, proper relationship.

Having ordered a couple of gin cocktails, we shamelessly snog some more in the sofa area of the next bar, like a couple of love-struck teenagers.

'You've lost an eyelash,' says Jake, gently picking one off my cheek.

Those BLOODY eyelashes. As part of my pre-date extreme sprucing, I decided to invest in a set of eyelash extensions. A little short of cash, I made the mistake of getting them done on the cheap with an online voucher.

I got what I paid for. Unfortunately, far from the natural fluttery look I desired, I came out of the salon looking rather like Widow Twankey in drag. Having been stuck on with some very cheap form of glue, probably Pritt Stick, they are now unashamedly MOULTING.

'Make a wish,' says Jake, holding the eyelash out on his fingertip. I shut my eyes and blow it off.

'Oh, you've got another one,' he says, reaching out to brush one off my cleavage.

'WISH GRANTED, HAR HAR HAR!' I cry.

At that moment, the barman calls out that they will be shutting in ten minutes.

'I can't believe it's gone half eleven already,' I grin as we walk out. I am feeling drunk with happiness (and, let's be honest, a lot of alcohol).

'I know,' says Jake, shrugging his jacket on. 'So . . . back to yours, then?'

I don't know why it shocks me so much. I don't know why it sort of hurts, a little bit.

Plenty of people sleep together on the first date. I, for one, have ploughed many a man on the first date. It's just that this time I thought it was different. I wanted so badly for it to be different.

So I grow a massive pair of chastity knickers.

'OOH, LOOK AT THE TIME!' I cry, gesturing in the direction of Big Ben, as if I can actually read the time on the bloody thing. 'Nearly midnight. I'd better be going!'

'Are you serious?' says Jake, looking decidedly put out.

'Yep, sorry, you know what they say. The early bird catches the worm!' I gabble. 'I'd really like to see you again, though?'

'Er, yeah. I guess we could hang out another time,' he replies, extremely unenthusiastically.

We walk back to the tube station together in awkward silence, the atmosphere and the magic completely shattered.

Back at my flat an hour later, I lie on my bed in absolute turmoil. It is all my fault. Why oh why, when faced with the one boy I actually really like and would probably have enjoyed having sex with, do I decide to turn into a bloody NUN? Am I a massive cock-tease for even kissing him in the first place? It goes against all my feminist principles, but at the back of my mind I can't shake the guilt that he has wasted time and money on me and not got anything out of it in return.

I awake next morning feeling unusually sober and refreshed, having for the first time in years had an early night on a Friday.

Immediately I reach for my phone. No message from Jake.

Hey! Had a great time last night, I type to him, knowing it goes wildly against the play-hard-to-get rule of dating, but too desperate by this point to care. *Did you get back okay?*

Three long hours later, during which I pace around the flat, psychopathically staring at myself in the mirror and shoving items of food into my mouth, my phone eventually pings with a reply.

Yeah . . . eventually. Ended up having to get two night buses though.

Oh GOD. Rather than earning Jake's respect by not sleeping with him on the first date and leaving him gagging for more, I have made him . . . CROSS.

In a fit of misery, I call and explain the situation to Danny, who I fear is in a somewhat frivolous mood.

'Send him a flirty message,' he says. 'Like "Hey big boy, how was your wank last night?"'

'Danny, no!'

'Too gay, you feel. Fine. Well if you want my advice, I'd just leave it. Mark my words, you'll be receiving a booty call in a few days' time.'

'How do you know?'

'Because I know dickhead guys. I'm one of them. Trust me, he'll be messaging you again. Thing now is for you to decide whether you're happy with a quick fuck, or whether you want something more.'

I hang up and sit for a few minutes staring at the background image on my phone. It's a slightly narcissistic photograph of myself in large sunglasses, gin bottle in hand and line of fags hanging out of my mouth à la Patsy from *Ab Fab*. At the time it was taken, on some drunken bender in Soho, this was the person I wanted to be. The fun, carefree, fuck-all-men image I wanted to portray to the world. But looking at it now, it feels … I don't know. Somewhat unsatisfying. And when things are unsatisfying, they normally turn out to be fake.

The usual me would have texted Jake again right now, apologising for my weird behaviour last night and seeing if he was free later, making it abundantly clear that tonight would have a very different outcome. In fact, the usual me would have woken up in bed with Jake this morning and would now be creeping to the bathroom to redo my makeup and glug water straight from the tap.

But something clicked in me last night. For those first few hours with Jake, I had a glimpse of what it might be like to be in a proper, adult relationship. To be with a guy who respects me and sees me as more than just a bit of fun. Someone who looks beyond the raucous exterior and falls in love with the person beneath. And I just can't seem to let that image go.

As it turns out, I end up sending a very different text.

Hey Mum – gonna come home a few days early, if that's okay.
See you later tonight x

Unlike Jake, she replies immediately.

Of course it's okay!! Have a safe journey sweetheart. See you
later xxxx

Call it a mother's intuition, or perhaps my complexion
being akin to that of a boiled turd, but as soon as I'm through
the front door that evening, she sits me down at the kitchen
table with a cup of tea (not, I note, a glass of gin) and asks if
everything's all right.

'I told you a bit of a porky last time I was home,' I mutter,
staring at my big toe poking out of the end of my tights. 'I
haven't really got a chap to bring to the wedding.'

She smiles at me fondly and takes my hand.

'Well, when Dad and I saw you on *Dinner Date*, we did
guess. Is there anything else the matter?'

I swallow down the lump forming in my throat.

'Do you remember Jake, that boy I really liked from drama
school?' I quaver, hot tears starting to plop down my cheeks.
'Well, we went out last night. And he's ghosted me.'

'Ghosted you?'

'Yeah, you know. When someone reads and ignores all
your messages, then pretends that you don't exist.'

'Goodness,' says Mum, putting her tea down in shock. She
looks at me searchingly.

Here we go, I think, cheering up a bit. You just can't beat
a good old-fashioned bit of motherly advice. Here is where
she'll throw in a comforting, ego-boosting lie, such as

that I'm too good for Jake and he is intimidated by my wit and beauty.

'Do you know,' she says, 'I thought ghosting was when you do a poo and it disappears down the U-bend before you've had a chance to take a look at it.'

Right. Well, not quite what I was expecting. Excellent.

'Dad and I don't care about you finding a partner, sweetheart,' she says, shuffling her chair round the table and drawing me in for a hug. 'All we've ever wanted, for you and your brother, is for you both to be happy.'

I smile, breathing in the familiar scent of Anaïs Anaïs perfume and the faint trace of grass cuttings. My mum.

'Besides,' she continues, 'look at your Auntie Marion. She's been single for fifty-two years and she's perfectly content!'

AAAGH.

14

The Wedding

© Sacha Miller

Five days later, I wake up in my childhood bedroom, with its 'Hickory Dickory Dock' wallpaper, bookshelf stuffed with old school textbooks, dressing table overflowing with hair scrunchies, dried-up pots of nail glitter and ancient bottles of Impulse body spray, and Pooh at the end of my bed (that's my stuffed toy Winnie-the-Pooh. Not a turd. Although I can see why the thought may have crossed your mind).

For a couple of seconds I am completely content, stretching out my toes and listening to the familiar racket of mooing and baaing from the field opposite. Then my consciousness kicks in. Oh, shit a brick. It's the day of the church rehearsal.

Feeling that I need serious fortifying for the day ahead, I head downstairs and straight for the gin cabinet. I say gin cabinet ... I have now learned to refer to it as the ELDER-FLOWER cabinet.

'Just pouring myself a refreshing elderflower cordial!' I say breezily to my parents, unscrewing the cordial bottle with my right hand while surreptitiously pouring Gordon's with my left. It is a skilful act that has taken many attempts to master. Like an alcoholic Jackie Chan.

'Are you sure that tonic water and limes really go with—'

'WHY YES, MOTHER! That's the beauty of elderflower ... it goes with everything!'

I then charge off to my bedroom before I can be questioned further.

I stare at my flushed and panting reflection in the mirror. This is it. Emma's final day as a free woman.

As I sit shaking on the end of the bed, rocking back and forth while glugging back the elderflower gin, it occurs to me that it's Emma who should be having the nervous breakdown rather than me. Yet she is probably calmly getting herself ready, eating a light and nourishing breakfast and cheerfully anticipating the day ahead, while I look like I should join the cast of *One Flew Over the Cuckoo's Nest*.

In traditional style, us bridesmaids will be sleeping over at Emma's house tonight and having our hair and make-up done together in the morning, something I am rather looking forward to. Shakily I start stuffing things into my overnight bag that I might need for the big day: toothbrush, toothpaste, hairbrush, Valium perhaps.

Hearing my parents head out for their morning dog walk – 'Frances! Frances! DO YOU HAVE THE POO BAGS?' – I slip downstairs and refill my glass, forgoing the elderflower this time and sloshing in two thirds neat gin.

By the time I'm ready to leave two hours later, I am a little on the sozzled side.

'Just off to the house of the Lord!' I call out cheerfully to my parents, heading purposefully towards the church, which is thankfully walking distance from the house. 'I'll see you tomorrow at the ceremony.'

'Are you sure you don't want me to drive—'

'TOODLE-OO!' I call with a backwards wave. Although this may seem a rather abrupt way to bid farewell to one's parents, I would like to point out that it's a distinct improvement on the time I drunkenly called out 'SICK NIGHT, BITCHES!' before hopping in a taxi to town, while they stood open-mouthed and apoplectic in the doorway.

I arrive to find Emma, Natasha, Louise and Ceri huddled outside the church, looking rather stressed.

'What's the matter?' I ask, hoping for an extremely disloyal moment that perhaps Emma and Sam have had a tiff and the wedding is off.

'Some idiot's managed to blow a fuse in the church,' Emma says. 'It's pitch-black in there.'

We wait for a further ten minutes while nothing seems to be done, then resort to lighting the place with the torches from our iPhones, making what should have been a beautiful, romantic rehearsal more like an episode of *Most Haunted*.

I can already feel a horrendous bout of 'church giggles' rising up inside me, a serious condition stemming from my school days. Something about the sombre atmosphere just completely sets me off. It doesn't help that wherever you look there are pictures of fat, naked cherubs and Bible readings littered with rude innuendo. For instance, that time when the vicar read out the story of 'The Miraculous Catch of Fish' and referred to Jesus 'seizing his tackle'. Or worse still, when the choir master at Llandaff Cathedral praised the head chorister, whose vast vocal range meant that she could switch between singing with the altos and the sopranos, by saying, 'The good thing about you, Elizabeth, is that you are a FLOATER!'

Now, our local vicar, Reverend Kitchen, is a lovely man, but one gets the impression that he is not actually a real vicar. More like an actor playing the role of a vicar in a Carry On film.

'Right, then!' he cries, rubbing his hands in excitement. 'Sorry about the light situation, girls, but I'm sure we can manage. Now, I'm going to start the service by revving up the audience!'

'The congregation, Andrew,' Jane corrects him. 'We're in the house of God.'

'Yes, that's the badger!' he beams, bounding up the aisle. 'And then I'm going to take to the stage—'

'The pulpit.'

'Yes, yes, the PULPIT . . .'

By this point, Louise, Ceri and I are finding it very hard to keep things together and have resorted to quietly crying tears of laughter behind our hymn books.

'Now then. Call me crazy, but I thought we could have a bit of fun with the vows. Emma, you'll say "I do". Then Sam will say "I do". Then, with a wink to the audience, all together we'll cry "WE DO!"'

'Um,' said Emma, looking pained, 'I'm not sure, Andrew. I wanted a more traditional service.'

'Oh, but it is traditional,' he replies, looking hurt. 'I saw it on *Don't Tell the Bride.*'

It is during the vows, when Reverend Kitchen instructs Emma and Sam to hold hands, adding, 'I'm a two-hander man myself!' that I completely lose it and have to go outside for some fresh air.

With the church rehearsal over, and Emma looking as though she could quite happily shoot herself, we all trudge back to her house for the night.

Unsurprisingly, a strict two-drink rule has been instigated by Jane ('There's nothing worse than a hung-over bride, Emma!'), so I have taken it upon myself to smuggle in a litre of vodka in an Evian bottle. Like a scene from *Malory Towers*, we then sit round in our matching pyjamas, sniggering and taking it in turns to have a swig. Natasha does not join in, instead painstakingly pinning her hair into Velcro rollers while glaring at us disapprovingly in the mirror.

We are sitting in Emma's old bedroom, a place where I spent half my childhood, and as I gaze blearily round, the memories come flooding back.

Dear God, the antics that went on inside these four walls.

There was the time when, aged seven, we laughed so hard at a ghost story we had made up – 'The Haunting of the Naughty Teapot' – that I actually wet myself and had to ask Jane for some spare pyjamas. Our elaborate games of truth and dare – like the time Emma dared me to go outside and walk barefoot across a bush. Which I did, then promptly fainted when I had to have a thorn pulled out of my toe. The pillow fight where I overzealously hurled a cushion through the air with all the strength of a male shot-putter, managing to take the bedroom light clean out of its fittings. Or the 'snogging scale' we made as fourteen-year-olds – a hideous piece of work detailing how far we had been with boys, ranging from a peck on the cheek to a cheeky finger. It was unfortunate that Emma accidentally wrote this on the back of a piece of religious studies homework that she later asked her mother to help her with. Apparently Jane exclaimed, 'Well, I expected it of Gabrielle, but not of you, Emma!'

Ah, fond memories.

With Louise and Ceri sleeping in the spare room, Natasha and I squash into Emma's bed, with Emma sandwiched in the middle. There is an unmistakable biscuity pong in the air, as the fake tan develops on our bodies. I always find that the smell of fake tan leaves me with a knot of nerves and excitement in my stomach, due to the fact that normally it precedes a date or a night on the town. Tonight, though, the stakes are far, far higher.

'I'm never going to be able to sleep,' Emma whispers.

A deep growl, like a bear on heat, signals to us that Natasha has had no such difficulties.

'You'll be fine,' I whisper back, wishing that I could sound more convincing. 'It's gonna be amazing.'

Please God, let it be amazing.

Finally, having bored myself to sleep by counting in my head the number of alcohol units I consumed that day (an alternative to counting sheep), the morning we have all been waiting for arrives. My own personal grievance at having spent almost an entire year trying and failing to find a date for the day pales into insignificance in the excitement of getting dressed and ready. There is also the dread of having agreed to give a reading in church. Being 'professionally trained', the weight of expectation on me to do this well is huge. The scrumpled copy sits in my handbag, covered in a mass of markings indicating breaths, dynamics and, of course, dramatic pauses.

In a blur of excitement we rush around taking it in turns to shower, the plughole soon blocked with a solid brown mush of leg hair and fake tan, before the doorbell goes, signalling the arrival of the make-up artist.

Volunteering to go last, so that I can smoke an entire packet of cigarettes outside while practising my reading, I head in an hour later to find the girls beautifully made-up with smoky eyes and their hair wound up into an elaborate arrangement of curls.

'Quick, Gabs, your turn,' says Emma. 'I need to go and get my dress on.'

Sitting on the kitchen chair with the make-up artist behind me, I feel myself relax, confident that I'm in the hands of a true professional.

The make-up artist, however, has other ideas.

'We've massively overrun and I'm meant to be at another appointment,' she informs me huffily, spitting her chewing gum out into a coffee mug. 'So I'm gonna have to rush you a bit.'

'Fine, fine,' I nod, getting the distinct feeling that this is not going to be fine at all. 'Just pop on a bit of contour and eye shadow.'

Ten minutes later, I look in the mirror and stifle a small scream. The make-up artist has indeed contoured my face. By gum, I have been contoured. So much so that I look like one of the contestants from *RuPaul's Drag Race*, but before their faces have been blended. Brown bronzer sits in random stripes across my face, in stark contrast to the dazzling white highlighter.

'Oh God,' I cry at my reflection. 'I look like a mint humbug.'

My eye make-up is somewhat worse – two heavy flicks of shadow sitting across my eyelids like dead ravens.

Here, I'm amazed to say, is where Natasha comes up trumps. Taking one look at my kohl-smeared face, she pulls me into Emma's bedroom, shutting the door behind us.

'Don't worry, Gabs,' she says, drawing out her own colossal make-up bag. 'I'll sort you out.'

I can't help but worry that this is some form of further sabotage and she's about to write 'penis' or 'I hate Emma' on my forehead in purple lipstick, but by this point I am beyond caring and let her get on with it.

'There you go,' she says, a few minutes later.

Wow. Looking in the mirror, I am amazed to see that she has actually done a blindingly good job, managing to soften out the eye make-up and tone down the harsh contouring on my face, adding a soft pink blusher to finish it all off nicely.

For a second, I don't know what to say, feeling a mixture of gratitude, embarrassment at this rare moment alone together and a touch of guilt at all the animosity that has built up between us. Although we've spent twenty years hating each other's guts, I can't deny that she's been a huge and important part of my life. And while we will never see eye to eye on most things (in particular, our differing interpretations of the word 'fun'), today we are united by the fact that we're both waving off our favourite person in the whole world.

'Cheers, Nat,' I say gratefully.

Luckily the atmosphere is broken by Emma coming out of the next-door bedroom with Jane fussing behind her. Shit. I mean, I may be biased, but my best friend looks achingly beautiful. Some people are just made to pull off a wedding dress, and Emma is one of them. I, on the other hand, would probably end up looking like a baked potato wrapped in a doily.

After a huge number of photographs, mainly from the professional photographer, but also from me barging through with my iPhone, us bridesmaids pile into a car and head down to the church. With the aid of magic knickers and a Wonderbra, I'm rather pleased with how my dress is looking. That is until I catch my heel on the back of it while walking across the grass bank, leaving a large muddy rip at the hem.

A crowd of onlookers have already gathered outside the gates, along with Reverend Kitchen, who is busy doing vocal warm-ups. Nervously we huddle together, clutching our little bouquets of flowers and awaiting Emma's arrival.

'Can ducks change sex?' pipes up the reverend behind me.

'P-pardon, Andrew?'

'Because I'm looking at that duck pond, see. And there were most definitely three girl ducks there last night. But now there's one girl and two boys.'

'Andrew, now really isn't the time for—'

'THE CAR WON'T START!' comes a sudden cry in the distance.

I turn to see Jane running down the hill, hand on her head to stop her large hat from blowing away. It turns out that the ancient Rolls-Royce hired to transport Emma to the church has given up the ghost right at the crucial moment.

'I know!' pipes up a helpful villager. 'It's all downhill from the house to the church . . . We'll push it!'

Horrific visions of Emma hurtling down the lane and straight into the duck pond flash before my eyes. Feeling the sudden need to pee, I desperately look around, wondering if I'll go straight to hell for peeing behind a gravestone.

I'm just preparing to hitch up my dress, thinking to myself, fuck it, I'm probably heading to hell anyway, when there's a great cheer and the Rolls-Royce turns the corner. Emma emerges, a smiling vision in white, linked arm in arm with her older brother, and after a hasty bit of veil-arranging and a few deep, shaky breaths (from me), we form a line and process into the church. (This, I must confess, makes me feel like something of a pillock, as it's that 'one together, two together' walk that makes you look like a one-legged pirate who's soiled himself.)

'Sorry,' I whisper, as I tread on the back of Louise's dress, nearly causing a pile-up.

Now, I am not a crier. I never have been. As a toddler, my parents took me to see *The Lion King* at the cinema. Apparently, the gut-wrenching scene where Simba's father dies caused me to burst into such raucous laughter that I had to be taken out.

But sitting in the church, watching Emma and Sam saying their vows, promising to love and look after one another till the end of their days, I suddenly find the floodgates opening.

'Dear God, what's happening?' I whisper to the girls, as snot violently cascades from my nose. The best man valiantly reaches for the handkerchief in his breast pocket, before realising that it is actually sewn in.

'And now Gabrielle will give a reading,' smiles Reverend Kitchen.

Oh fuck. Why did I agree to this? I look at the reverend with a mixture of panic and hysteria before blowing my nose in my bouquet and climbing the pulpit.

'Once upon a time, there was a boy who loved a girl,' I begin in a shaking voice. 'And her laughter was a question that he wanted to spend his whole life answering.'

I then proceed to make a strange strangled sound, somewhere between a honk and a moo, before stumbling through the rest of the poem and collapsing back in my seat.

That's why Gabrielle can't get any acting work, I imagine everyone thinking to themselves. She's absolutely terrible.

So that is it. Emma and Sam have tied the knot. Months upon months of preparation over in the blink of an eye. Before we know it, we are all pouring out into the sunshine, throwing confetti over the newly-wed couple (mine unfortunately gets stuck to my sweaty palm and ends up being thrown over myself).

'That vicar was brilliant,' beams my father, standing waiting at the gates. 'We've already booked him for your wedding.'

'OH HA DE HA HA,' I reply crossly, heading off in search of booze.

It is a dazzling reception. The world's biggest marquee, decked with flowers, candles and copious amounts of champagne. My parents, to their delight, have been seated at a table with the Reverend Kitchen and his wife. At each table, Emma and Sam have very sweetly placed a large bottle of flavoured vodka and a line of shot glasses, for everyone to toast the speeches with. As soon as we sit down, I hear the reverend call out, 'Let's crack this bad boy open then!' before racking up a line of shots, which to my amazement he and my parents knock back. Jesus. They're going to be even more wasted than I am.

Sam has written such a moving speech about how he and Emma met – describing how she used to run away from him in Bridgend, throwing her chips at him and telling him to fuck off – that she has to read it for him while he sits drying his eyes at the table.

There is also a blinder of a slideshow, including a rather embarrassing photo of me sitting fully clothed in the bath clutching a bottle of red wine. Followed by one of my red thong that I lost on the hen do being publicly returned to me.

Watching Emma and Sam on the dance floor, drunkenly hollering Ed Sheeran into one another's faces, I'm filled with a contentment that I haven't felt in a long while. A realisation, if you will. It isn't my turn yet. One day, hopefully, I'll find him: a nice, cheerful sort of chap with good levels of personal hygiene and preferably a dab hand in the kitchen. A man who'll catch my eye and proceed to sweep me off my feet (although actually, given past events, hopefully he WON'T sweep me off my feet. I can't cripple another one). But right now, it simply isn't my turn.

This is unfortunately the last coherent thought I have, as following the two portions of hog roast that I consume in front of my horrified parents (who still believe I am a staunch vegetarian), I pass out stone cold at the buffet table.

God knows what I'm dreaming of, but when someone
wakes me with a cry of 'Gabby, get up! It's Emma's wedding,
for God's sake!' I reply with 'IT'S IN THE CUPBOARD
UNDER THE KITCHEN SINK' before passing out again.

> My dearest Pegleg,
>
> In the words of Mr Bennet in *Pride and Prejudice*,
> 'I cannot believe that anyone could deserve you.
> But I heartily give my consent.'
>
> Or perhaps a W. C. Fields quote would be
> more appropriate: 'Everybody's got to believe in
> something. I believe I'll have another beer.'
>
> Your faithful hound,
> Bitchtits xxx

Six months later

It's 2 a.m. and I am once again banging on the front door of my parents' house.

'Muuum!' I call through the letter box, swaying precariously and nearly nose-diving into a pot plant. 'I don't have my keeeys!'

My mobile rings.

'BITCHTITS!' hollers Emma. 'Shit, forgot you were staying at ours! Left without you!'

'Shfine,' I slur, as my mother silently opens the door before heading back to bed. 'I'll get a lift to yours tomorrow and collect my car.' I let out a little sicky burp as I cannon off into the kitchen.

'Soz, Gabs. Fucking steaming. Oh my God, did you get that guy's number?'

'Who, DECLAN?'

I stick my head in the kitchen sink and drink directly from the tap, letting the cool water run down my face and soak my bra.

'I could look past the gold tooth and the tattoo of a spread-eagled naked lady, really I could,' I continue, coming up for air. 'But when he informed me he was on PAROLE for attacking someone with an umbrella, I decided it was a step too far.'

'Shit, yeah,' Emma replies, making disgusting loud chewing noises.

'What you eating?'

'Chips. Got the taxi to stop off.'

'Emma, for fuck's sake, mun, you're dripping curry sauce all over the bed!' comes Sam's voice in the background.

'Jealous,' I say, removing a block of cheddar from the fridge and taking a bite directly from it. 'Good night though, wasn't it?'

'The best,' says Emma. 'So glad you came down. Gonna go sleep now. Na-night, Gabs, love you.'

'Night, love you too.'

I stagger up the stairs to my bedroom and sink into bed, the room revolving. Despite my pounding headache and the feeling that I'm about to projectile-vomit over my cuddly toy collection, a smile creeps its way across my face.

Some things will never change.

Acknowledgements

I'd like to say a HUGE BLOODY THANK YOU to everyone who made this book possible.

To my loyal blog readers, whose tweets, comments and shares got me here in the first place.

To my fantastic editor Hannah Boursnell, amazing agent Laura Williams and all the team at Sphere – for all your hard work and for making the whole process such ruddy fun.

To my insane and wondrous circle of friends – thank you for believing me when I told you I had a book deal and not just assuming that I was sat at home, watching daytime television for eight months.

And finally, to the funniest two people I know – my incredible Mum and Dad. Thank you for your unwavering support and for turning a blind eye every time I have a fag out of my bedroom window. Love you.

Additional Credits

Kate Stone for the 'Black Or White' song lyrics

Debrett's A–Z of Modern Manners by Bryant, Corney and Massey (Debrett's Ltd, 2008)

The Ladies' Book of Etiquette and Manual of Politeness by Florence Hartley (Hesperus Press, 2014)